Snippets of Life

Florence E. Adams

TRILOGY CHRISTIAN PUBLISHERS

TUSTIN, CA

TRILOGY

Trilogy Christian Publishers
A Wholly Owned Subsidary of Trinity Broadcasting Network
2442 Michelle Drive
Tustin, CA 92780

For information, address Trilogy Christian Publishing

Rights Department, 2442 Michelle Drive, Tustin, Ca 92780.

Trilogy Christian Publishing/ TBN and colophon are trademarks of Trinity Broadcasting Network.

For information about special discounts for bulk purchases, please contact Trilogy Christian Publishing.

Manufactured in the United States of America

Trilogy Disclaimer: The views and content expressed in this book are those of the author and may not necessarily reflect the views and doctrine of Trilogy Christian Publishing or the Trinity Broadcasting Network.

10 9 8 7 6 5 4 3 2 1

Library of Congress Cataloging-in-Publication Data is available.

ISBN 978-1-64773-212-7

ISBN 978-1-64773-213-4

Contents

Contents

Introduction

Footprints. As we go through life, we have an impact on the lives of others. Whether good or bad, we all leave footprints. These footprints are evidence that we've touched someone else's life. I pray that the footprints I leave are first encouraging and then edifying. I pray that I have helped someone along the way. I might have made bad choices and bad decisions, but maybe, just maybe, by being transparent, I have helped someone not to make the same mistakes. I also hope to have inspired someone to feel like going on, to never give up, and to hang in there.

I titled this book *Snippets of Life* because God gave me the word *snippets*. I came to understand "snippets" as being little pieces of wisdom, like the small pieces of paper the fall to the floor when you snip the edges off of a paper snowflake. Although they vary in size and shape, if you stretch your imagination you can still use them productively. And you'll discover that even the tiniest snippets are usable. Every time you trim a piece off while making your snowflake, you're actually cutting off a snippet. These snippets are the footprints of life that I'd like to impart to you, to help you make it through whatever you're facing in life. Remember, as you go through difficult times, you're not alone.

God has given me a voice and insights to share that will help make this journey we call life just a little easier. This book is called *Snippets **of** Life*, not *for* life, because I'm sharing little pieces of my life. I am trying to help make your life just a little easier and perhaps a little better.

When titling this book, I considered the title *Snapshots of Life*, but the problem with a snapshot is that it is stationary; it never changes, it is permanent. *Snippets* proved to be a more logical choice, because you can change a snippet. As it is with life, a snippet is ever-evolving, ever-changing. Although you may find yourself in a difficult situation, it doesn't have to stay that way; it can change and evolve. You can decide if it changes for the better or for the worse, but it will change; it will not remain the same. So, by allowing you into my life, you can see how the decisions I've made and the actions I've taken changed my situation and influenced the outcome of that situation. In addition, they have made me a better and stronger person through my Lord and Savior, Jesus Christ.

No-Win Situation

When you find yourself facing what you feel to be a no-win situation, look to Jesus. In times of distress and despair, things are not always as they appear. While you're going through your situation, you may think you are facing it alone or that no one understands, that no one cares. How could anyone possibly understand what you're going through or what you're feeling? They're not going through this; it's not happening to them. We tend to focus on the here and now and not the total picture. We stress out, we drink, we cuss, and we run amok, racing here and there with no real course of action nor any real solution or tangible outcome in mind. We even use quaint cliques to help us feel better equipped to handle our situation, such as: "It's always darkest just before the dawn"; "Every cloud has a silver lining"; and "What doesn't kill you makes you stronger." Although we say these things, we don't believe them, and we continue to search for comfort.

The Scriptures tell us that God won't put more on us than we can bear:

> No temptation has overtaken you except what is common to mankind. And God is faithful; he will not let you be tempted beyond what you can bear.
> —1 Corinthians 10:13

In addition, all things work to together for those of us who love the Lord and are called to fulfill His purposes:

> And we know that in all things God works for the good of those who love him, who have been called according to his purpose.
> —Romans 8:28 NIV

We are also called to look to the Lord for our help:

> I lift up my eyes to the mountains—where does my help come from? My help comes from the LORD, the Maker of heaven and earth.
> —Psalm 121:1–2 NIV

"Jesus will work it out," we say, "and the Lord will make a way." At church and when talking to other

Christians, they tell us to "just pray about it. If you're going to pray about it, then don't worry; but if you're going to worry, then don't pray." Let's be real. I agree wholeheartedly with these promises, but the problem is, when I'm going through a situation or I'm dealing with difficult circumstances, I don't want to hear these things. You may be able to relate to this feeling. At that point, we're broken, hurt, or disappointed, and we are not ready to embrace these truths. Notice I said that we are "not ready." Don't misunderstand or get me wrong: I know that God doesn't put more on us than we can bear. I also realize that all things, no matter how painful, distressful, or difficult, will work out for the good in the end. In addition, I know that by looking to the hills from whence cometh my help, I am merely looking to Jesus:

> *Fixing our eyes on Jesus, the pioneer and perfecter of faith. For the joy set before him he endured the cross, scorning its shame, and sat down at the right hand of the throne of God.*
> —Hebrews 12:2

But for the here and now, I want to deal with that person or situation that is causing me so much pain and agony. Or in some instances, I'd rather not deal with that person or situation at all, depending on the circumstances, and I simply choose to ignore it.

I know that the Lord will make a way, regardless of the circumstances, situations, and people who are involved. I know that prayer changes things, situations, and people, but during my situation, depending on where I am in it, I just don't want to hear someone telling me that all I have to do is pray. I want someone to tell me that they have my back. I want someone to be outraged with me. I remember going through a painful situation and a friend told me, "Let's handle this and pray about it later." At that time, that's what I wanted to hear. Even though we didn't follow through with the threat, the words felt good to hear. It felt good to feel like I still had some control over the situation, and that I wasn't alone.

When we feel like we're in a no-win situation, there are several things going on. For starters, we have no or very little control; the element of surprise has taken control, and we're in a state of utter disbelief. We find ourselves gripped with the fear of the unknown, asking ourselves what's next. We wonder what else is going to happen. Or even worse, we ask ourselves what else can happen. When everything around us seems to explode with malfunctioning confusion and dissimilation—in other words, when all hell breaks loose and everything that could and would go wrong seems to be going wrong—we're left feeling stunned and mesmerized. The realization that we are not in control is real, and most of the time it is very painful. But here's the real question: Were we ever really in control in the first place? Let's face it. When we're in what feels like a no-win situation, we're out of our element, our comfort zone, and it scares us to death. So, what should we do about it? What can we do about it? During these times, Satan will throw every fiery dart in his arsenal at us to keep us off balance. He will pummel us with doubt and defeat, trying to attack our minds. Satan will even try to attack our heart—but don't give up and don't give in.

Here's a thought. Why not try trusting, leaning, and depending on God? Jesus tells us that rather than fear, we must believe:

> *Overhearing what they said, Jesus told him, "Don't be afraid; just believe."*
> —Mark 5:36 NIV

It can't be said any plainer than that!

The second thing that happens in a no win-situation is that we struggle with timing. The timing of a difficult situation is always wrong and inconvenient. These things *always* strike at the most inconvenient time—not that there's ever a good time to have a problem or be in the midst of a no-win situation. But you will notice that these things usually occur when we're ill-equipped to handle the situation. For example, final notices seem to always come between paydays. We often find ourselves spinning our wheels, and then discovering that our wheels are turning but we're still getting nowhere fast. Occasionally, we overthink and overstate the problem, and we become exasperated to the point of total dissatisfaction and utter frustration. That is when some people turn to drugs, gambling, drinking, unhealthy and unrealistic relationships, and crime, often leading to addictions or prison time, and we are left in a worse situation than our current one, with even more confusion, complexities, and complications. In the worst-case scenario, destruction and death are the outcomes of a no-win situation.

So, when it feels as though we are in a no-win situation and our backs are against the wall, we must stand. God has got us covered, and He has our back, even when it doesn't feel like it. God is so big that He can cover the whole world with His love, and He is so small that He can curl up inside your heart. Nevertheless, we have to trust and believe, even when we don't feel like it. We are to encourage ourselves during our times of struggle:

Be filled with the Spirit, speaking to one another with psalms, hymns, and songs from the Spirit. Sing and make music from your heart to the Lord, always giving thanks to God the Father for everything, in the name of our Lord Jesus Christ. Submit to one another out of reverence for Christ.

—Ephesians 5:18–21

Remember, God didn't bring us this far to leave us now.

Typically, when we acknowledge God during our no-win situation, the situation changes, and it doesn't feel as devastating. We start discovering a path forward that we didn't know existed, or help comes unexpectedly.

The good news is that even in your no-win situation, God is at work. His power and His love are ever-present. Use the acronym *SUBMIT* to further understand how to acknowledge God:

S: Seek God. This requires going to God in prayer, studying His Word, and asking Him what you should do, how you should handle the situation: "You've tried the rest, now it's time to go to the best."

U: Unleash God's power in you and your situation.

B: Believe that God will do just what He said He would do.

M: Motion: We are to put God's answers and direction into motion (practice). Remember, without God you cannot, and without you He will not.

I: Interact! Remember what God has already done in your life. Be a witness, give your testimony, and interact with other saints.

T: Thank God for your yesterdays, your today, and your tomorrows:

- Thank Him for the things He's already done.
- Praise Him for the things He's doing.
- Worship and honor Him for the things He's going to do.
- Be steadfast and give Him all the praise, honor, and glory.

The Bible says this in 1 Corinthians 15:58: *"Therefore, my beloved brethren, be ye stedfast, unmoveable, always abounding in the work of the Lord, forasmuch as ye know that your labour is not in vain in the Lord"* (KJV). So, remember, if God doesn't do another thing for us, we already have plenty of reasons to thank Him. We can never thank God enough, even if we had ten thousand tongues.

Thank God for the Good, the Bad, and the Indifferent

We should thank God for the good times, the bad times, and the indifferent times. It's easy to thank God for the good times, and we can learn to thank Him for the bad times, during our trials and tribulations. It's the indifferent times that have the greatest potential to create growth in us. In these times of indifference, God blesses us, promotes growth, gives direction, and provides guidance. The indifferent times are those times when things aren't clear-cut. Indifferent times takes the good, adds the bad, and equals the whatever. During these times, we're left wondering if we should run to the hills or hide low in the valley. The irony is that often these times of indifference are thrust upon us through no fault of our own. We find ourselves in indifferent times because of the actions or inactions of others.

During times of indifference, we often wonder exactly what's going on. We may think, *Was it something I did? Was there something I could have or should have done differently? What did I do to cause this? What can I do to change this? How can I fix this?* We may even begin to question God: *God, can You hear me? Where are You? Have You turned Your back on me? Have You removed the hedge of protection from around me? God, why can't I hear You?* And more to the point: *God, why does it hurt so bad?* We must always realize that the hand of God is present during the good times, but His hand is there especially in the bad times, and He is there even in the indifferent times.

When God leads us to the edge of the cliff, we must trust Him fully and let go. Only one of two things will happen: Either He'll catch us when we fall, or He'll teach us how to fly!

During this time, some of us find ourselves in a state of emotional chaos, struggling with right and wrong, good and evil. Paul wrote, *"I find then a law, that, when I would do good, evil is present with me"* (Romans 7:21 KJV). That's when we have that little devil on one shoulder and an angel on the other shoulder. The little devil is berating us, creating doubt, giving us a sense of fear, and trying to destroy all the good we're doing—because that's his job. The Bible tells us in John 10:10 that *"the thief cometh not, but for to steal, and to kill, and to destroy: I am come that they might have life, and that they might have it more abundantly"* (KJV). This is the time when the little devil is speaking louder than the angel, and he's telling us to get even, to seek our own satisfaction, to get revenge. However, we must not give in. Vengeance does not belong to us:

> *Dearly beloved, avenge not yourselves, but rather give place unto wrath: for it is written, Vengeance is mine; I will repay, saith the Lord.*
> —Romans 12:19 KJV

During this time, the struggle we are experiencing is spiritual warfare. The Bible tells us that *"we wrestle not against flesh and blood, but against principalities... against spiritual wickedness in high places"* (Ephesians 6:12 KJV). And again, we find ourselves questioning God. The problem is not that God has left us, but that we've strayed away from Him. God is a Spirit, and those of us who worship Him must worship Him in Spirit and in truth (see John 4:24). Here's the good news: There's no struggle that God can't see us through, and there's no question too big or difficult for God to answer. The Bible tells us that *"God understandeth the way thereof, and he knoweth the place thereof"* (Job 28:23 KJV). Loosely interpreted, this says that only God understands. Only God knows the way to wisdom. God is the source of wisdom, and He reveals it to us. Psalm 111:10 declares: *"The fear of the LORD is the beginning of wisdom: a good understanding have all they that do his commandments: his praise endureth for ever"* (KJV).

So, no matter what circumstances you find yourself in, whether it is good, bad, or indifferent, always thank God. First Thessalonians 5:18 instructs us: *"In everything give thanks: for this is the will of God in Christ Jesus concerning you."*

Not Good for You

Have you ever been in love with someone who wasn't in love with you? Or worse yet, have you ever been in love with someone who not only was not in love with you, but who wasn't good for you, either?

When a person isn't good for you, everyone seems to recognize it except you. Although there are many tell-tale signs, you choose to ignore them, because you want what you want, who you want, when you want it, and nothing or nobody is going to stand in your way.

What are some of the signs that a person isn't good for you? Usually the person is manipulative, self-centered, self-serving, and conniving. Often, they will stop short of nothing to get what they want. Most will attempt to separate you from anyone who may truly love you, including your family; this isolates you. They want you all to themselves, and they will do anything to get it that way. They will attempt to take up all your free time—your every waking minute—if you will allow them to. The key words here are "if you allow them to"; no one can do anything to you unless you allow it.

We often hear people say that love is blind; personally, I think love is not only blind, but it is stuck on stupid. It has one leg with a kickstand, so that every time you try to stand up, all that person has to do is kick the stand right out from under you and whoops! You're back in love again. The average person won't walk away even when they figure out that this is not the person or relationship for them. Oftentimes we're too busy making excuses, trying to turn a bad relationship into a good one, trying to force that person into being the right person for us.

We often tend to stay in unhealthy relationships due to financial security or gain, for sex, because we are in love, or even just to say we are in a relationship. All of these reasons are sure to lead to disastrous endings, but for the time being, they justify and satisfy our particular desire.

One true sign that the person is not good for you is that bad things happen to you when you're with that person, such as suddenly having legal issues when you've never had legal problems before, or fighting with siblings beyond the occasional sibling rivalry. Chaos erupting around you is a bad sign. Everywhere you turn there's something going wrong, warning signs, red lights, horns, and bells. I used to say that when it came to me and my relationships, God had to speak to me with neon signs and flashing lights, and I still might not get it. Perhaps it was because I chose not to see it because I wanted what I wanted at that time. Remember, all things in life are based on the choices we make.

It's also possible that you have an unexplained gut feeling that the person isn't right for you. You can't really explain it or put your finger on it, but it just doesn't feel right. Can you say *intuition*, or better yet, the *Holy Spirit*? My cousin told me once, concerning her relationship with a new partner, that she "didn't fit." I didn't fully understand her at first, but then I came to realize she didn't feel as though she fit in his arms or his life well. Something didn't feel right, and if she didn't fit, then how could she be comfortable and secure in the relationship? How would he protect her? Later she began to understand why she didn't fit: He was a fraud and a womanizer. Sometimes something just doesn't agree with you; the feeling can be strong or it can be subtle. Unfortunately, we often don't see for ourselves that something is wrong, because we're in love.

When someone is not right for you, they can get you hurt or killed; a prime example is David and Bathsheba. They can bankrupt you both emotionally and financially, much like what happened in the parable of the prodigal son:

> And the younger of them said to his father, Father, give me that portion of goods that falleth to me. And he divided unto then his living. And not many days after the younger son gathered all together, and took his journey into a far country, and there wasted his substance with riotous living. And when he had spent all, there arose a mighty famine in that land; and he began to be in want. And he went and joined himself to a citizen of that country; and he sent him into the fields to feed swine. And he would fain have filled his belly with the husks that the swine did eat: and no man gave unto him.
>
> —Luke 15:12–16

They will assassinate your character and ruin your reputation. They will drag you down. Your life will drastically change from where you once were, soaring with the eagles; now you're hanging out with turkeys—or worse, you find yourself waddling in a pigsty. And then there's the ultimate price you could pay...death.

So, how can you know if a person isn't right for you? How long does it take to realize that person is not right for you? What would be some of the warning signs?

What can you do, if anything, to keep yourself from entering into these types of relationships?

Let's start with how you would know. As I mentioned before, intuition or the Holy Spirit plays an important role in relationships. That feeling you have, pay attention to it. It's not there for no reason. I've been told on several occasions that a woman knows when her man is cheating; no one has to tell her; she can just sense it. Some of us tend to ignore those feelings. Stop ignoring them. I learned out of experience that that saying is right.

Then there are other people who will try to tell you what they know about the individual. I have always said that everyone has a past, and we should leave their past in their past. I wouldn't let anyone tell me anything. That was mistake number one, because I was wrong, and had I listened to what other people tried to tell me, I could have saved myself a whole lot of heartache and a great big headache.

Look at the relationship for what it is. Be honest with you. Ask yourself what you want out of the relationship. What exactly is it that you like about this person and why? Where do you see the relationship going? Where would you like the relationship to go?

As women we tend to have blinders on when it comes to our relationships. We need to remove them!

We chase men, sleep with men, accept lies from men, and allow the wrong men to trample all over us. Quit giving these men all your power! Even though a relationship is give-and-take, don't be the one making all the concessions.

Moreover, for both men and women, stop looking at the window dressing. Here's the problem with choosing a mate based on the window dressing: Looks fade, bank accounts are temporary and they dwindle, and jobs come and go, especially in today's economy. What is the window dressing? Window dressings are those superficial things that we believe makes a person a perfect mate. For some, window dressing includes appearance, religion, education, culture, economic status, employment, and other benefits and rewards. Don't get me wrong, these factors are important, but only in their proper place.

My ideal mate is God-fearing and God-loving, at least six-foot-five or taller, handsome, educated, cultured, financially stable, and working at a job with benefits and perks. However, what's more important than any of those things is how he treats me. How does he make me feel? Does he make me smile and laugh? Does he challenge me to be all I can be and more? Does he take time to communicate with me? What does he have to say? Is he polite, courteous, and respectful?

How long does it take to figure out if a person is the right person for you or not? That's a fair question; unfortunately, there's no right or wrong answer. We each discover it at different times. I asked a few of my friends, and I heard everything from "a few weeks" to "three to four months." Realistically I can't say because it's all based upon where you are mentally, emotionally, spiritually, and even financially. We all eventually get there; it's just a matter of when.

What are some of the warning signs that this person is not the right person for you? I don't pretend to know them all, these are just a few suggestions of things to look out for. Listen to his conversations, for out of a man's mouth his heart speaks; at least that is what the Bible says:

> A good man out of the good treasure of his heart bringeth forth that which is good; and an evil man out of the evil treasure of his heart bringeth forth that which is evil: for of the abundance of the heart his mouth speaketh.
>
> —Luke 6:45 KJV

Also pay attention to the way he treats you; watch his facial expressions and body language. Evaluate the relationship. Are you disagreeing about almost everything because of different ideas, beliefs, and values? Is he suddenly too busy to spend time with you? Has he stopped doing the things he used to do? If so, why? Does he always want to go hang out with "the guys," often leaving you alone? Does he need a lot of "me time"? Does going out to dinner create a fight? What type of vibes is he giving off? Ask yourself if he is spending time with you because he wants to be with you. Or is he just doing time, in a relationship with you just to "pass the time," or merely satisfying you so that you'll quit asking about it? When you call him, is he always too busy to talk to you? Do you always have to be the one calling him because otherwise you won't talk? Does his cell phone ring repeatedly and he hits the ignore button to keep from answering it? On the other hand, does he answer it and pretend it's his friends or a family member when it's obvious that he is talking to another woman? Maybe he is having low-pitched, secretive conversations in the bathroom, in the car, or in another room and he suddenly hangs up when you enter the room. Maybe he leaves the phone in the car or turns it off when he is around you. Does he always have an excuse as to why he didn't show up or didn't bother to call? Do you find yourself doing more of the giving and less or none of the taking in the relationship?

What can we do about it if we discover we are in a relationship that is not good for us? Some people just stop talking. Occasionally, people stop answering the phone calls, but often we nonchalantly start becoming unavailable. We begin doing other things, such as starting an exercise regimen, taking up a new hobby, or doing something else that will take our focus in another direction, away from the failing relationship and its problems. Some people just walk away. Splitsville—they're gone. Sometimes the split is amicable, but other times it could be equated with WWIII. However, whether you are male or female, you must learn to bow out gracefully. That person's circumstances could change, and you might discover that they are actually what God intended for you but they just had to get some things together first.

What can you do, if anything, to prevent yourself from entering into a bad relationship? First and foremost, ask God if this is the right mate for you. If not, ask Him to send you the right mate. Second, communicate more with the person; start asking questions. Don't be so eager to jump into a relationship. Take your time; if that person was meant for you, they'll still be there. If they are not there, then maybe you just saved yourself a lot of regret.

Remember, what God has for you is for you, and no hell or high water can prevail against it. Pay attention to what he says and how he answers your questions; also pay attention to what's not being said. If his is not good with financial issues, don't give him power over your finances. Observe him in a different way, looking for the warning signs early. Examine yourself, see what needs to be changed or made better, and then change your attitude.

Let's break the cycle! Start trusting God. God knows what's best, and He'll give you what you need.

> *Thou preparest a table before me in the presence of mine enemies: thou anointest my head with oil; my cup runneth over.*
>
> —Psalm 23:5 KJV

All you have to do is ask and believe. Ask Him for what you want, John 14:14 states, *"If ye shall ask any thing in my name, I will do it"* (KJV). Believe God to do exactly what He said He would do. The Word of God tells us: *"The grass withers and the flowers fall, but the word of our God endures forever"* (Isaiah 40:8 NIV). So, regardless of what you may think, God's got this. You simply need to ask. The Word says in Matthew 7:7: *"Ask and it shall be* given you; seek and ye shall find; knock, and it shall be opened unto you" (KJV).

Behind the Mask

When you feel like you're at the end of your rope, what do you do? Commit suicide, murder someone, take drugs, drink, or sleep around? Exactly what do you do? You can't run fast enough, you can't sleep enough, you can't eat enough to feel better, and you don't have enough money to buy your way out of the situation. So, what do you do?

You put on your fake face and your fake smile and you go into character. You start pretending that everything is okay, that life is full of nothing but joy. But deep within, you realize that with every breath you take, you're slowly dying inside.

We all wear masks, but to the person who feels like she's at the end of her rope, the mask is a vital and essential part of her being. The mask hides all the hurt, pain, disillusionment, worry, and disgust. The mask is very deceptive within itself, sometimes adding intrigue and even charm to the individual. It can be amazingly beautiful, or mesmerizingly frightful, sparking curiosity in others because they want to know what makes the individual tick.

So, exactly what is behind the mask? Behind the mask is a little girl or little boy fighting to escape all the pitfalls of life, all the wrong friends, the wrong men or women, and the wrong decisions they have made. They are hiding from all the pain they felt from years of hurt and abuse, along with fears of inadequacy and purposelessness. Behind the mask is a troubled man or woman whose only discourse to a world of tears is motivated by the need to be accepted and loved.

When we look behind the mask, we delve into the psyche that demonstrates great cynicism with statements such as "I'm worthless. Nobody loves me; nobody wants me." Behind the mask, they fail to realize that they are a remarkable person.

When we are hiding behind the mask, we don't see all the people who care about us and look up to us. Behind the mask, our outlook is so bleak that we fail to see the person whom God intended for us to be. Behind the mask is great turmoil and anguish. Behind the mask is a frightened individual who is working hard to please others, concerned only with what others say and think. So, what is behind your mask?

The big question is how to remove the mask. Removing the mask requires a lot of prayer, growth, and insight as to who we are. Removing the mask is a process, slow and tedious, because we have to remove one layer at a time. This requires us to look deep within, examine ourselves, and learn to accept our faults and failures as well as our strengths and successes., realizing that it takes all these things to make up who we are and who we've become.

We are never to go back, but we are to look back so we can make the appropriate changes necessary to make our lives better. We need to see all the things that God has brought us through, all the blessings He has bestowed upon us. How He has protected us from dangers seen and unseen, and how He sometimes had to let us run into the proverbial brick wall so that we'll realize that it hurts. Some lessons have to be learned the hard way, because no matter how many times someone tries to keep us from hitting that wall, we insist on running straight into it.

How many times has someone tried to get us to see that someone is no good or not right for us, and yet the more they warn us, the more we run to that very individual? Oftentimes we get angry with the person trying to help us, telling them "to mind their own business," or dismissing their warnings by saying, "They don't know what they're talking about." Deep down inside we actually know that they are right, but we just won't admit it.

Sometimes we feel as though we can't admit it because by admitting it we must admit that we made a mistake and that we really don't know everything after all. Then, when chaos erupts, we go back to that same person and say, "Why didn't someone stop me?" or "Why didn't someone tell me?" Really? Come on, you didn't want to know or see because you thought you knew best at the time.

Once we remove the mask, we can stop being superficial. We can let out all the things that have hindered us from being able to enjoy life, and we can begin to see all the beauty that has been bestowed upon us. We become transparent and lose the spiritual amnesia from which we all tend to suffer. We begin to see the marvelous creations that God has called us to be. We remove some of the negativity from our lives, and we strive to see the best in others as well as ourselves. After removing the mask, we understand the remarkable joy of being God's greatest creation.

Once we remove the mask, we no longer are people pleasers, but we prefer to be God pleasers. Once we remove the mask, we don't care what others think and say about us as much as we care about what God says and what we think and say about ourselves. We come to recognize the sad truth that we can spend our entire life trying to please someone else, only to discover that it'll never be enough. When we remove the mask, we find inner peace and joy. The quality of our lives becomes richer and purpose-fulfilled. When we remove the mask, we can see God.

FLORENCE E. ADAMS

Trusting God

While I was enjoying an exhilarating worship service one Sunday morning, a song was sung that resonated deeply within the recesses of my mind and spirit. The song, which spoke of trusting God, resided within me for several days. Why? Because it was talking about totally relying on the Lord, not just when things are going well, but trusting Him when things aren't going so well. We all know it's easy to trust and believe in Jesus when things are going well. But what happens when things are going haywire and all hell breaks loose? Do you or will you still trust God?

When I was married, I thought the sun rose and set on my husband. I knew he *could* do wrong; I just wouldn't believe that he *would* do wrong. I had him so high on a pedestal that even he couldn't measure up. I took the vow that said, "Forsaking all others, cleave unto your husband" literally. And then all hell broke loose. One day while washing our clothes, I found a letter written to him by another woman. Things got worse. I began to find other letters and pictures, and I noticed he was staying out all night. I thought my life had ended.

I am a creature of habit, and before, I had always run to church when all hell broke loose in my life. This time something was different. This time I wanted to die. Yes, I had three children who depended on me, but I'd never felt so alone in my life. I was miles away from home, with no family, no real friends, and this person whom I had held so highly was now discarding me, throwing me away... I didn't know where to go, how to fix it, or what to do. I went through every emotion known to man. I felt like a failure because I couldn't make my marriage work. I was a firm believer that marriage was meant to be forever, but mine was failing.

I cried and I prayed, trying to understand how this could be happening to me. I tried everything I could think of to become what I thought he wanted. I called some of my so-called friends for advice. And I even unknowingly tried witchcraft (upon the advice of a "friend"), to no avail. I was doing all of this while still going through the ritual of attending church. The Bible warns us to guard our heart:

Above all else, guard your heart, for everything you do flows from it.

—Proverbs 4:23 NIV

The Bible also warns us to watch what we allow to enter into our hearts and our spirits. I suddenly began to understand that others shouldn't easily lead us, that we need our own minds, our own states of consciousness. Jesus supplies us with the Comforter, the Holy Spirit, to guide us:

> Howbeit when he, the Spirit of truth, is come, he will guide you into all truth: for he shall not speak of himself; but whatsoever he shall hear, that shall he speak: and he will shew you things to come. He shall glorify me: for he shall receive of mine, and shall shew it unto you.
>
> —John 16:13–14 KJV

I decided to run away, and so I packed up my belongings and my children and I moved. That didn't help, because he followed me. He showed back up in my life, openly flaunting his cheating behavior, but I still kept trying to hold on because I couldn't grasp the idea that maybe my marriage wasn't going to last forever.

Finally, I began to get fed up with the situation. I began not to care so much about my circumstances, but I came to understand that God was still in control and that He was going to take care of the situation. I didn't even know what it was that God was going to do, but

I just believed He would do it, no matter what it was! Don't get me wrong, I was still praying. I was praying for God to restore my marriage back to where it had been, because I didn't know how I was going to make it without this man. I knew what I wanted, but I was too blind to see that God had a better plan for me. Isaiah 55:8 says, *"For my thoughts are not your thoughts, neither are your ways my ways, saith the LORD"* (KJV). I had to surrender. I had to relinquish my will to God's will. I had misplaced my trust; I had begun to idolize my husband, putting him before God. I had broken the number-one commandment, *"Thou shalt have no other gods before me"* (Exodus 20:3 KJV). I had made my husband my god. Finally, I realized that I was so far down that I didn't have anywhere else to go but up.

That's when God started to speak, and I was ready and willing to listen. He had been talking all along; I just didn't want to hear what He had to say. Now I was seeking His face and opening my spiritual ears to hear and my heart to understand what He was saying. The time had come, and now I was all ears. He spoke to my spirit, telling me to let my husband go. I didn't completely understand this, but I trusted that everything would be fine. I was practicing Proverbs 3:5: *"Trust in the LORD with all thine heart; and lean not unto thing own un-*

derstanding" (KJV). So, I let him go. I signed the divorce papers and trusted God.

God was working even though I couldn't see it. I still held on to my faith and the belief that God was in control. I didn't like what I had to go through at the time, but it was all worth it in the end. Proverbs 3:6 says, *"In all thy ways acknowledge him, and he shall direct thy paths"* (KJV). One year after the divorce, I bought my first new car. Three years later, my student loan was paid off. That same year I bought my house, with no money. I literally had no money, but it was all God. I came to understand that although I was trying to hold on to my husband, on whom I had depended for so long, God had another plan. He removed my husband from my life so I could grow spiritually and depend solely on Him. And when I did, he gave me everything I needed. He said in His Word that He would supply all our needs.

I learned to trust God. Psalm 62:8 says it best: *"Trust in him at all times; ye people, pour out your heart before him: God is a refuge for us"* (KJV). God had been working behind the scenes all along, even when I couldn't see Him and wasn't even seeking Him.

Wanting People Who Don't Want You

We are all victims of playing the fool at one time or another. We are willing to chase, lie, steal, and kill just to get a little attention or affection from that certain someone. We run around like little puppy dogs, leaping and jumping at every opportunity to be in their presence. The pursuit of love will make us do some very foolish, dangerous, damaging, and silly things. What won't we do for love? How far will we go? What will we give up? These are valuable questions, but unfortunately they are without answers, because until you cross that line, you don't know exactly what you'll do, how far you'll go, or what you are ultimately willing to give up.

Look at Samson and Delilah. Samson gave up everything. Samson didn't go into the relationship blindly or lightly; he knew exactly what he was getting into. He gave up:

- God's presence with him:

And she said, The Philistines be upon thee, Samson. And he awoke out of his sleep, and said, I will go out as at other times before, and shake myself. And he wist not that the LORD was departed from him.

—Judges 16:20 KJV

- His sight and his freedom:

But the Philistines took him, and put out his eyes, and brought him down to Gaza, and bound him with fetters of brass; and he did grind in the prison house.

—Judges 16:21 KJV

- His self-respect, as he was greatly and cruelly humiliated:

And it came to pass, when their hearts were merry, that they said, Call for Samson, that he may make us sport. And they called for Samson out of the

*prison house; and he made them sport: and they set
him between the pillars.*

—Judges 16:25 KJV

Love can make us reckless, wreaking havoc every-where we go. It can make us wish at times that we had never met the person, in an effort to avoid the awful awakening of unwantedness. It propels us into another dimension, causing us to profoundly lose our minds. All sane thoughts are out the window, giving way to chaos and confusion, and creating great difficulties in how we relate to others, especially those whom we al-lege to care about. Love can be just plain ol' relentless.

Sadly, once love bites you in the behind, you feel as though you can't live without that person from whom you have received this affliction. Yes, I said *affliction*, not *affection*. So often we hear of the bad things that oc-cur when someone says, "If I can't have you, no one else will." The individual can't and/or won't accept that the person doesn't wish to be in a relationship with them. Occasionally, they take matters into their own hands and injure or kill the object of their affection or the in-dividual whom they think is standing in their way. We see this in our everyday lives—just pick up a newspaper or watch the news. We can see it in the Bible, too, when

Uriah, Bathsheba's husband, was killed by King David so that he could be with her (see 2 Samuel 11:15).

It doesn't matter your race, creed, color, or your financial, political, social, or religious status, we all have at one time or another experienced rejection. Personally, I've witnessed some of these instances. In one case, the individual was killed while trying to force his then-ex-girlfriend, who had filed an emergency protective order against him, to go with him against her will. Another instance took place when an ex-boyfriend attempted to kill her new love interest, stabbing him eighteen times, because the woman had chosen this new man over her ex. Both incidents were tragic to say the least, but both could have been avoided had the individuals just accepted the fact that they weren't wanted by their love interests.

God always gives us a way out, but we don't always take it. First Corinthians 10:13 says it like this: *"No temptation has overtaken you except what is common to mankind. And God is faithful; he will not let you be tempted beyond what you can bear. But when you are tempted, he will also provide a way out so that you can endure it"* (NIV).

Why, then, do we seem to want the people who don't want us? Why do we keep pursuing these ill-fated relationships? Is it psychological, neurological, or just plain stupidity? When a person doesn't want you, there's nothing you can do or say that will force them to. They simply don't want you. James 4:2 says, *"You desire but do not have, so you kill. You covet but you cannot get what you want, so you quarrel and fight. You do not have because you do not ask God"* (NIV). We are supposed to ask God for everything, including our mate, but so often we think we know best. And then we choose an individual ourselves, trying to make them fit the image of our heart's desire, even though that person may not be the one whom God has in store for us. This leads to the mess we call love.

If everyone would just be honest, a lot of these problems wouldn't occur. Both parties need to be honest with one another. We must quit lying and making statements like "I'm not looking for a relationship. I just want to be friends. I just want somebody I can talk to," knowing that we are, in fact, seeking a relationship. We just want to be around that person so much that we lie.

Good communication is the key, and this goes for all relationships. In my personal relationships, the only thing I ask of a partner is for them to just be honest and let me know if he is no longer interested or no longer wants to be bothered. At that point I'd gladly walk away. Jesus said, *"If anyone will not welcome you or listen to your words, leave that home or town and shake the dust off your feet"* (Matthew 10:14 NIV). I'm not equating myself with Jesus, but I've got sense enough to know that if you don't want me, then you don't want me, and there's nothing I can do about it but walk away. Pestering someone about it, or even trying to hurt them, will not make them want you. It'll only make them pity, hate, or despise you.

It is difficult when a person fails to recognize the fact that someone doesn't love them or want them. Many of these people are left feeling broken, tarnished, disposable, and just plain ol' unwanted. The most difficult thing to watch, as a family member or friend of such an individual, is that no matter what anyone says, when it comes to matters of the heart, they will not listen. They just can't let go and move on. They insist that the person they long for shares their feelings or is returning those same feelings back to them. No matter what happens, it's always someone else's fault, or they accuse everyone of misunderstanding the situation. To everyone else it is clear that the other person no longer wants to be bothered with or by them. Moreover, most of them will do anything to keep that person away, but to the love-starved and unwanted person, these are just temporary feelings, or they believe someone is meddling and trying to keep the two of them apart. Nothing could be further from the truth, but let's face it, they're too far gone to recognize it.

So, there you sit, frustrated and confused because you suffer from loneliness, wanting someone who doesn't want you. What are you going to do about it?

What most of us discover is that once we get the object of our affection, it's not what we expected. We end up disappointed. Many times, we find out that they look better as window dressing, and that every relationship comes with a price. Upon closer observation, we begin to see all the things we had chosen not to see: nasty attitudes, mean spirits, and flaws. Mr. or Mrs. Right isn't so right after all. The grass always looks greener on the other side until you get close enough to see the weeds. If you are smart, you won't have to experience pain to realize this is not the person for you or the person you thought they were.

Love is blind, and it makes us blind. Some of us experience pseudo-love—not necessarily love, but lust that we call love, or some of us just love the feeling of being in love. Just as Samson and David had to learn these lessons, we have to learn them as well. Samson paid the ultimate price—he paid with his life.

And Samson called unto the LORD, and said, O Lord God, remember me, I pray thee, and strengthen me, I pray thee, only this once, O God, that I may be at once avenged of the Philistines for my two eyes. And Samson took hold of the two middle pillars upon which the house stood, and on which it was borne up, of the one with his right hand, and of the other with his left. And Samson said, Let me die with the Philistines. And he bowed himself with all his might; and the house fell upon the lords, and upon all the people that were therein. So the dead which he slew at his death were more than they which he slew in his life.

—Judges 16:28–30 KJV

David, on the other hand, paid with the death of his firstborn son, whom he fathered with Bathsheba (see 2 Samuel 12:18).

What did you have to give up? What did you lose? If you only lost money or time, you came out virtually unscathed. You walked away with your life.

According to the Bible, real love doesn't hurt. Real love is kind and gentle; real love is patient and honest. The Bible says in 1 Corinthians 13:4–8 (NIV):

Love is patient, love is kind. It does not envy, it does not boast, it is not proud. It does not dishonor others, it is not self-seeking, it is not easily angered, it keeps no record of wrongs. Love does not delight in evil but rejoices with the truth. It always protects,

always trusts, always hopes, always perseveres.
Love never fails.

What do you do when the person you want doesn't want you? First, you must acknowledge that you are somebody and that you are worthy of being loved. You deserve better than a messed-up ideology of love, and you won't settle for less. You now fully understand that half a man or woman is not better than none at all. You are a whole person, and you need a whole mate. If you choose to be single, know that one is a whole number; you don't need a mate to complete you. You're already complete in Christ (see Colossians 2:10). My ideology is that my mate should accessorize and complement me, not complete me.

I once told my ex-husband that I should never need him; I should want him and desire him, but I should never need him to be in my life. I need God, and I wanted my husband. I still believe and live by that rule. You must begin to realize that you are a valuable and lovable human being. You must know that you are seated with Christ in the heavenly realms (see Ephesians 2:6). You deserve to be treated with dignity and respect. You are pretty or handsome in your own way, because that's how God designed you to be. Ephesians 2:10 says this: *"For we are his workmanship, created in Christ Jesus for good works, which God prepared beforehand that we should walk in them"* (KJV). Begin to focus on who God made you to be. Know that God loves you, and that Jesus died for you (see 2 Corinthians 5:15). Acknowledge that you are special because you are a gift from God.

> *Every good and perfect gift is from above, and cometh down from the Father of lights, with whom is no variableness, neither shadow of turning.*
>
> —James 1:17 KJV

If someone rejects you, it's their loss and not yours. That person lost the opportunity to have you impact their life. Once you make these realizations, everything else will fall into place.

Self-Pride

One of the things that I tried to instill in women whom I met while traveling with my husband, who was in the military, was that you should always command and demand respect. No one, regardless of who it is, has the right to treat you any less than respectfully. When you walk into a room, your mere presence—the way you walk, talk, dress, and present yourself—should command that you receive respect. And when you open your mouth, you should demand respect, not by saying the words, "I demand respect," but by what you have to say. I was taught as a child that when I entered a room, I should greet everyone who was already present in the room; a simple "hello," "good morning," "good afternoon," or "good evening" will suffice. Most of the time someone will return the greeting. If something is going on in the room, don't interrupt; just go in quietly and sit down immediately. There will be time at the end of the gathering to be polite, to socialize, and to discover what you might have missed. Be courteous, be attentive, and speak only to ask a question, if it is the time set aside for questions, or when called upon. Always exhibit patience, consideration, confidence, and self-pride; be neat in your appearance and not loud and vociferous. Be seen by your presence, not by your noise. My philosophy has always been not to be loud to be seen, but to have my presence be enough.

I've come to the realization that in order to demand respect, first you must love yourself. How do you expect someone else to love you if you don't first love yourself? How do you expect to give love if you don't know how or if you have never learned to love yourself? You must first love yourself before you can love anyone else. Secondly, you must respect yourself. Respect for yourself must come from within. If you do not respect yourself, no one else will. If you don't care about you, why would anyone else care about you?

I wish for each of you to know this, to feel it in your spirit. You are valuable; you are not to be abused in any way, not physically, not emotionally, not spiritually, and not sexually. You are God's workmanship:

> *For we are his workmanship, created in Christ Jesus unto good works, which God hath before ordained that we should walk in them.*
>
> —Ephesians 2:10 KJV

You are beautifully and wonderfully made:

I will praise thee; for I am fearfully and wonder-
fully made; marvelous are your works, And that
my soul knows very well.

—Psalm 139:14 KJV

Don't let anyone tell you differently! Do not accept any words meant to demean and dehumanize you. You are more than those words; you are more than a conqueror (see Romans 8:37). You are not a second-class citizen; you are a first-class citizen, and you don't have to put up with mess. You are a citizen of heaven, and you are significant (see Philippians 3:20). Although you can't control what someone calls you, you can control what you answer to. You are the head and not the tail:

The LORD will make you the head, not the tail. If
you pay attention to the commands of the LORD
your God that I give you this day and carefully fol-
low them, you will always be at the top, never at
the bottom.

—Deuteronomy 28:13 NIV

You are to be respected and loved because you are God's child (see John 1:12). And guess what? You are worth it. You were created not to walk behind your man to be led by him; nor were you created to walk in front of him to lead him. You were meant to walk by his side.

> So the man gave names to all the livestock, the birds in the sky and all the wild animals. But for Adam no suitable helper was found. So the LORD God caused the man to fall into a deep sleep; and while he was sleeping, he took one of the man's ribs and then closed up the place with flesh. Then the LORD God made a woman from the rib he had taken out of the man, and he brought her to the man.
>
> —Genesis 2:20–22

You were meant to be his helpmeet.

You don't have to fear rejection, criticism, or secrets from your past. Let your past be just that—your past. God has cast your past transgressions into the sea of forgetfulness:

> For as high as the heavens are above the earth, so great is his love for those who fear him; as far as the east is from the west, so far has he removed our transgressions from us.
>
> —Psalm 103:11–12 NIV

You have been redeemed and forgiven:

> *For he has rescued us from the dominion of darkness and brought us into the kingdom of the Son he loves, in whom we have redemption, the forgiveness of sins.*
>
> —Colossians 1:13 NIV

Let go of the luggage of yesterday. Release yourself from all your hurt, pain, disappointment, and failure. Think of these things as lessons learned: Some lessons you will pass on the first try; others you have to repeat; but thank God you will make it through. Be confident that the good works that God has begun in you will be perfected (see Philippians 1:5). Life has so much more to offer you; give yourself permission to love and to move on. Forgive yourself (see Psalm 51:10). God already has forgiven you (see 1 John 1:9). You are the only one who is holding you back.

Someone e-mailed me a poem named "How to Recognize a Good Woman." I searched for the author and discovered it to be unknown. However, I still found this poem to be profound, and I think it speaks volumes to us as women. Although it doesn't cover everything that we as women are exposed to and must deal with, I still find it pertinent for this conversation.

How to Recognize a Good Woman

A good woman is proud of herself.
She respects herself and others.
She is aware of who she is.
She neither seeks definition from the person she is
    with,
Nor does she expect them to read her mind.
She is quite capable of articulating her needs.

A good woman is hopeful.
She is strong enough to make all her dreams come
    true.
She knows love; therefore she gives love.
She recognizes that her love has a great value
And must be reciprocated.
If her love is taken for granted, it soon disappears.

A good woman has a dash of inspiration,
A dabble of endurance.
She knows that she will, at times,
Have to inspire others to reach the potential God
    gave them.
A good woman knows her past,
Understands her present, and moves toward her
    future.

A good woman knows God.

She knows that with God, the world is her playground,

But without God she will just get played.

A good woman does not live in fear of the future because of her past.

Instead, she understands that her life experiences are merely lessons,

Meant to bring her closer to self-knowledge and unconditional self-love.

FLORENCE E. ADAMS

Thrown Away

Have you ever felt thrown away, discarded, rejected like disposable trash? You did all you could do, said all you could say, and gave all you could give, and it still wasn't enough. Relationally, spiritually, and emotionally, you're drained. You've become exasperated with defeat.

For many years I tried to overcome just this feeling, reaching for acceptance in an unaccepting, frigid world. I tried to escape the agonizing pain, but it just wouldn't go away. No matter what I did, it still loomed. It still hurt! I couldn't be good enough, bad enough, or just plain ol' enough. I felt as though I was blessed with a curse. The curse, which is really a blessing, is that I'm a giver, but worse than being a giver, I'm a giver who is trying to get.

At around the age of five, I was told that I was an accident, and that my sister was wanted because I was selfish. I'm the older sibling, and yet I constantly lived in the shadow of my younger sister. No matter what I did, no matter how much I gave, it just wasn't enough. I'm not jealous of my sister; I just wanted to be accepted for me. I couldn't understand why I wasn't good enough, why no one wanted me, why I wasn't enough for someone to want. I began to rationalize that if I tried very hard, and if I stayed out of trouble, then I would be accepted, but what I found instead was more hurt and disillusionment.

When I was in my early teens, my maternal grandmother decided in her infamous wisdom to reiterate this feeling. She told me that my mother didn't want me, and that my mother had tried to give me to her. So there I was in my teen years, a time already filled with confusion, insecurities, and other problems, and not one, but both of my grandmothers told me at different times and on different occasions that I'd never amount to anything, nor would I ever have anything.

My fraternal grandmother went as far as to say just before my wedding day that getting married was going to be the best thing I ever did. This is the same woman who was notorious for giving me a compliment and then immediately snatching it back. She'd say things like, "You would be a pretty girl if you'd lose weight." And I would understand that my beauty was based on my size. Both of my grandmothers had a personal problem with my mother, for one reason or another, and I was their scapegoat. Their way of inflicting pain on her was not only to reject and hurt her but also to reject an hurt my sister and me. I thank God that my story didn't end there. I can truly say that without God on my side, I don't know where I would be. God kept placing other adults in my life who encouraged me, influenced me, and guided me. He kept and sustained me, just as the Bible says in Psalm 121:4: *"He who watches Israel will neither slumber nor sleep"* (NIV). Based on my circumstances, I really didn't have any reason to achieve anything or believe in myself.

Then I got married, and wow, that ship took me around the world and back again, literally and figuratively. I've lived all over the world, and after a failed marriage, I'm back. Getting divorced made me feel like I was being tossed away again. That's a whole another story, but that is when the questions began again: *What's wrong with me? Why is it that no one wants me? What do I keep doing to make people throw me away? Why does everyone leave me?* There are times when I felt like I had no real friends, I had no man in my life, and my family only came around when they wanted or needed something.

I've been thrown away so much that I now see it as normal. Once I've served my usefulness, then I know what's coming next. I live by the code that if I had as many people pushing me to succeed as I do who are waiting for me to fail, I'd have it going on. I'm suspicious of anyone who tries to get too close; I begin to wonder what their angle is. What do they want? And Lord forbid they say those magic words, "I'll never hurt you," or any variation of those words—wait for it, wait for it... Whoops, there it is, I'm suddenly thrown away. I know that's it coming; no, I don't look for it, but it's coming. *What is wrong with me?*

The greatest irony of all is that God gave me the gift of encouragement, to help others see that God hasn't given up on them and that they shouldn't give up on themselves either. Now tell me that God doesn't have a sense of humor. The person whom everyone has thrown away is supposed to encourage others. God has allowed me to encourage others in many different aspects of life, and by encouraging others, oftentimes I'm encouraged, too. God will give you exactly what you need, just when you need it.

I can relate to loners. Someone once told me that he was a loner who didn't like to be alone, and I adopted that statement as my own. So, if you ask me to describe myself, I would repeat that same sentiment: "I am a loner who doesn't like to be alone." The person who told me that used it as a pickup line or a come on; I, on the other hand, feel as though it's become my way of life.

God is such a good God that He placed people in my life at all the pivotal points. I know that people are in your life for a reason, a season, or a lifetime. I now understand that some seasons can feel like a lifetime, especially when things are bad. And they can feel as short as a solar eclipse when things are good. What can be worse than feeling like someone's leftover trash?

I had a person tell me to quit bellyaching, that my memories and experiences were nothing, so I should just get over it. What I discovered is that when you're broken, no one can tell you how long you're allowed to feel hurt, insecure, and scattered. There's no magical chart that says:

- For feeling thrown away: It should only hurt for five days.
- For being physically abused: It should only hurt for fourteen days because that's how long it should take you to heal.
- For being mistreated: It should only last two days because it's not like you were physically abused or anything.
- For hurt feelings: It should only hurt for ten minutes. It's only words—you act like someone killed your dog or something. Get over it!
- For mental abuse: Since it's all in your mind, if you change your mind it'll go away in a day or so.

- For spiritual abuse: No one should be able to abuse you spiritually. If they did, then your faith is just not strong enough. (Basically, it didn't happen.)

Feeling thrown away helps me to warn others to be careful of how they treat people. Hebrews 13:2 warns us: *"Be not forgetful to entertain strangers: for thereby some have entertained angels unawares"* (KJV). I often remind them not to give up on anyone or throw anyone away, because God didn't give up on that person or thrown them away. I know that sometimes you have to love people from afar, but you still can't throw them away. I explain to them that Jesus met them where they were, and that no one is beneath us. We can't afford to look down on anyone else; instead we should be extending a hand to lift them up. We must also be careful of the bridges we burn because somewhere along the way, we'll most likely have to travel across that same bridge again. Am I my brother's keeper? The answer is an unequivocal *yes*.

I've learned that God doesn't make mistakes and He doesn't create junk. I now know that I wasn't an accident or a mistake; I am a gift from God. Therefore, you and I, we are both gifts from God, and we each have a divine purpose (see Colossians 1:9–12). I'm safe in the knowledge that God knew me before I was born, for Jeremiah 1:5 declares: *"Before I formed thee in the belly I knew thee; and before thou camest forth out of the womb I sanctified [set apart] thee, and I ordained thee a prophet unto the nations"* (KJV). I also know that I am fearfully and wonderfully made (see Psalm 139:14). I find comfort in knowing that I was set aside for His will. I know that no matter what family, friends, or others may say, Jeremiah 1:8 tells me: *"Be not afraid of their faces: for I am with thee to deliver thee, saith the LORD"* (KJV). God is the Author and Finisher of my faith.

God can mend your broken heart. He can take away the pain. It's not easy to believe, because the pain is great, long-lasting, and real. The effects are often so devastating that it feels as though God, too, has walked away. Then I remember that God is not a man. He cannot and He will not lie:

God is not a man, that he should lie; neither the son of man, that he should repent: hath he said, and shall he not do it? or hath he spoken, and shall he not make it good?

—Numbers 23:19 KJV

He has shown me that I could then, and I can now, stand on His promises. He reminds me that nothing can separate me from His love:

> For I am persuaded, that neither death, nor life, nor angels, nor principalities, nor powers, nor things present, nor things to come, nor height, nor depth, nor any other creature, shall be able to separate us from the love of God, which is Christ Jesus our Lord.
> —Romans 8:38–39 KJV

He lets me know that I am established, anointed, and sealed by Him:

> Now he which establisheth us with you in Christ, and hath anointed us, is God; who hath also sealed us, and given the earnest of the Spirit in our hearts.
> —2 Corinthians 1:21–22 KJV

He'll do exactly what he said He will do and then some:

Now unto him that is able to do exceeding abun-
dantly above all that we ask or think, according to
the power that worketh in us.
—Ephesians 3:20 KJV

God will open windows in heaven and pour you out
a blessing that you won't have room enough to receive:

Bring ye all the tithes into the storehouse, that
there may be meat in mine house, and prove me
now herewith, saith the LORD of hosts, if I will not
open you the windows of heaven, and pour you out
a blessing, that there shall not be room enough to
receive it.
—Malachi 3:10 KJV

He's faithful; He will never leave you nor forsake
you:

Let your conversation be without covetousness; and
be content with such things as ye have: for he hath
said, I will never leave thee nor forsake thee.
—Hebrews 13:5 KJV

It ain't over until God says it's over. My pastor taught
me not to put a period where God has placed a comma.

So, keep your head up, and keep trusting and believing in God. My God is the possible in the midst of the impossible. Impossible is God saying, "I'm possible—try Me!" All things are possible with God—just believe (see Matthew 19:26)!

> *As soon as Jesus heard the word that was spoken, he saith unto the ruler of the synagogue, Be not afraid, only believe.*
>
> —Mark 5:36 KJV

Think about it: You're in good company. Jesus was thrown away. No matter how much good He did, the so-called good people still threw Him away. They condemned Him to death, nailed Him to the cross, pierced His side, and ridiculed Him. And after all that, He gave up His life freely.

When You're Tired of Hurting

Have you ever felt like if one more person hurts you, you'll just roll over and die? Surely God didn't form you to go through this much hell-on-earth. Surely, when He decided to breathe the breath of life into your lifeless form, He had other ideas, thoughts, and aspirations for you and your life. I know that He didn't design me to be other people's punching bag or dumping ground; there just has to be more to life than that.

So, we pray and pray, begging and pleading for an answer: "God, why did You make me? Why are You allowing so much hurt and pain in my life? What did I do to deserve all of this?" Sadly, it can seem as if God has turned a deaf ear, that He can't hear us. So, we wait, hoping things will get better, waiting tearfully for an answer that never comes. Therefore, we muddle through life, trying to fade to black. By fading to black, we are blending into the background, hoping that no one will notice us, because if no one notices us, then no one can hurt us. On the other hand, we find ourselves desperately trying to fit in—where we are not wanted and more than likely don't belong.

Some people turn to drugs, some turn to alcohol, others sink devastatingly into depression, but all seek a release from the pain, agony, and emptiness that they feel every day of their lives. We discover that we can't talk about our feelings to anyone because then we're said to be wallowing in self-pity or having a pity party, when we're actually just a wounded soul pleading to be heard. Where does the hurt go? It goes inside until it builds to a boiling point of seismic proportions, and then either explodes or implodes. Either we act out, or we're drugged out. We are acting out and doing things totally out of character, or we have a total meltdown and end up hospitalized, medicated, and sedated.

Suddenly we begin questioning our self-worth. Are we worthy of being loved? Yes, of course, we are, but also in this state of mind not only do we not realize it, but we also can't even fathom it. Being found worthy escapes us. Our hearts and minds are in so much turmoil that we fail to realize that we are not only worthy but that we deserve to be loved as well. In all the chaos and confusion, we deem ourselves unlovable or incapable of being loved, when in fact it's just the opposite.

So, what do we do? We go on pretending until we realize the problem is not with us, but with the people we have around us. Then we realize we have to let go of some people and some things and move on. It's not easy, because most of the time, these people have been in our lives for a long time or they are our family members. While writing this snippet, I was talking to my daughter about letting people go. We agreed that some people, no matter how long the relationship has lasted, just are not worth holding on to. Then my daughter said something profound: "Look at the people in your life and ask yourself whether you would trust them with your most prized possession, your child(ren)." I had to pause for a moment and think of the people I've called friends, then I asked myself if I would trust them with my children. My list was already short, but with that it became even shorter, and I started deleting phone numbers and de-friending people on Facebook. Looking back, I realize that these were the people who had hurt me the most, but because we had been "friends" for so long, I kept hanging on to them. Why did I hang on to these destructive friendships? I had become comfortable and complacent in my relationships, and I was used to all the drama surrounding them. Yes, it hurts to let them go, but after the hurt comes the healing. And in most instances, we realize that we're so much better off without them in our lives.

Love is not supposed to hurt, so why do we continue to let other people continually hurt us? Remember, when someone has a problem with us, it's their problem, not ours.

Most of us can handle the hurt when it comes from a stranger, but when the hurt comes from a friend or a family member, the betrayal can seem unbearable, and it can give way to feelings of desperation, disillusionment, and total despair. There's a saying that applies here: "The closest does the mostest." It's the element of surprise that hurts the worse, because these people are supposed to care for us, protect us, and be there for us, not be the source of our pain. Yet they are the very ones who are distressing us, humiliating us, and destroying us.

One of the problems, in most instances, is that we give these individuals the ammunition to hurt us. We tell them private, intimate details of our lives, and then they use that information later to berate us and betray us. Or we give them the power of influence, and they influence us to do things that are totally out of character for us. This again gives them more ammunition to use against us. Perhaps they backstabbed you while you were in a relationship so that they could have the man or woman you were with, or otherwise betrayed you.

The question is: What are we going to do about it? Should we hide, preferring to stick our heads in the sand? Should we run down the street sounding the alarm of injustice? Or should we fight, preferring to stick up for our lives and ourselves? Normally, that's when the law of self-preservation comes into play. The law of self-preservation states that we are naturally instilled with a fight-or-flight mechanism, and when we find ourselves in a dangerous situation, it's only natural for us to either run or to stand and fight. Occasionally we do both: We run for a while, but then we stop and begin to fight.

So, how do we fight? First, we fight with the Word of God. The Bible tells us to put on the whole armor of God (see Ephesians 6:11). So, how do we do this? We do this by the life we live, as a living, walking testimony. We let others see "the Word" in action in our lives. Secondly, we take a stand and face the situation head-on. Thirdly, if needed, we get others involved. The whole concept is to fight, at all cost, letting nothing and no one stop us. If they persist on hurting us, they don't need to be involved in our lives, especially not as a part of our inner circle.

Therefore, what is the process of alleviating the hurt? We begin alleviating the hurt one step at a time. First, we must identify what's hurting us. Secondly, we must apply the Word of God to the hurt. Then we must begin to change the situation, by having a change in our mind, breaking away from those hurting us, and finally moving on to a new journey or adventure. We must realize that it is okay to speak with others about what's hurting us, because oftentimes it feels taboo to speak with others about these things. Of course, we can't talk to everyone. We have to take into consideration that people have their own problems and don't want ours weighing them down or complicating their lives any more than they already are. Occasionally it is best to go talk with someone who doesn't know us, such as a counselor, a therapist, or a spiritual leader whom we know is inspired and led by God. Whatever you decide to do, do something that is in alignment with the Word of God. The key is to do *something*. I've learned that writing is the best therapy I could have ever tried. I know that I'll be judged and that by putting it in print, it's now permanent—but it's healing to me. I finally have a positive release from the hurt, pain, and frustration. Find your positive release. It may come through writing, drawing, or cooking, for example. Try to write or keep a journal or start drawing or cooking. Find your niche, whatever it may be, to release all that's built up inside. Where God guides, He provides, and who knows? I may be reading your book one day or buying a piece of your art or perhaps eating in your restaurant.

The Words of My Mouth

Let the words of my mouth, and the meditation of my heart, be acceptable in thy sight, O LORD, my strength, and my redeemer.

—Psalm 19:14 KJV

I've recited this prayer hundreds of times when I was a child, as a closing prayer after children's choir rehearsal, at a young women's missionary meeting, at Baptist Training Union (BTU) services, and countless other times in various organizations. However, I never thought about what I was really saying.

Let the Words of My Mouth...

Let us examine this phrase for a moment. First Peter 4:15 says, *"But let none of you suffer as a murderer, or as a thief, or as an evildoer, or as a busybody in other men's matters"* (KJV). Our words speak life and death, and when we indulge in these words, we eat the fruit of them. Too often we underestimate the power of a smile, a kind word, or a kind act.

And the Mediations of My Heart...

Our nature comes out of our mouths. Remember, our temperament is our way of dealing with life. So, if I understand this statement completely, what's in my heart comes out of my mouth. Wow! So, if my heart is cold, then what I say will be cold and calculating, but if my heart is warm, I'll show compassion and mercy. What does your heart have to say?

Jesus gave us the recipe in Exodus 30:22–25 (KJV) for what our nature should be and how we are to live our lives:

> Moreover the LORD spake unto Moses, saying, Take thou also unto thee principal spices, of pure myrrh five hundred shekels, and of sweet cinnamon half so much, even two hundred and fifty shekels, and of sweet calamus two hundred and fifty shekels, and of cassia five hundred shekels, after the shekel of the sanctuary, and of oil olive an hin: and thou shalt make it an oil of holy ointment, an ointment compound after the art of the apothecary: it shall be an holy anointing oil.

Liquid Myrrh
The recipe calls for 500 shekels of myrrh.

Sweet-scented Cinnamon
The recipe calls for 250 shekels of cinnamon.

Fragrant Calamus
The recipe calls for 250 shekels of calamus.

Cassia
The recipe calls 500 shekels of cassia.

Olive Oil
The recipe calls for a hint of olive oil.

Myrrh + Sweet-scented Cinnamon + Fragrant Calamus
+ Cassia + Olive Oil = A holy and perfumed oil.

Just as babies must learn to talk, we must learn to
speak God's way. We are supposed to encourage, exhort, and bring edification everywhere we go. Our
words are powerful, and depending on how we choose
to use them, we can build people up or tear them down,
we can encourage and support, or we can discourage
and disparage.

We do have choices on how we use our words. Sometimes we don't realize that our words and behavior may be perceived by others as meanspirited, callous, or degrading. The tongue is like a double-edged sword; it cuts both going in and coming out. The Bible says in James 3:8, *"The tongue can no man tame; it is an unruly evil, full of deadly poison"* (KJV). How do you use your words? When was the last time somebody spoke a kind word to you? How did it make you feel? Think about how you come across to others. What words do you use?

Oftentimes we use words without fully understanding what they mean. Take, for instance, the word *exhort*. In the Greek language, the word *exhort* (*parakleto*) means "to call near," and *exhortation* means "to invite comfort." Therefore, exhorters bring comfort into other people's lives. *Parakletos* means to encourage, strengthen, help to inspire, and comfort. So, we need to watch what we say to and about other people. Don't be the devil's mouthpiece. The word *slander* in the Latin translates as *scandalum*, and in the Greek it translates as *skandalon*; both mean "trap." *Slanderer* in the Greek is *diabolist*, which means "false accuser, devil." So be careful of falling into the devil's trap.

Our verbal communication includes our choice of words, our tone of voice, and our volume. What have you said today? Did you exhort, or were you the devil's mouthpiece? Some things, people say, you have to take with a grain of salt and think about who's speaking. Most people will say we should consider the source. But think about it. What is their motivation for saying what they are saying? Is it to help or improve, or is it designed to hurt and hinder? Life should not be, and it is not, at least for me, garbage in and garbage out. Did you take the time to build someone up? Or were you tearing someone down? Here, let's make it plain: Were you an encourager, or were you a gossip? There's a saying: "Loose lips sink ships." Did you sink someone today, or did you throw them a life jacket and help them up?

More important than what we say about others, however, we must watch what we say to and about ourselves. No person's words have more impact or as much authority in our lives as our own. Speak life and not death. Say things like "I am a beautiful queen," not "I'm too fat," or "My nose is too big." Say "I can do all things through Christ who strengthens me," not "I can't do anything right." Encourage yourself by saying things like, "No weapon formed against me shall prosper," not "The man is holding me down." Or say, "I'll give this a try, and if it doesn't work, I'll try something else" instead of "This will never work. I'm such a failure," which leads to negativity, self-doubt, and eventually depression and defeat.

The Bible tells us to use our words wisely, to only speak when we have something encouraging or edifying to say, not to just talk to hear ourselves talk, silly chitter-chatter. Proverbs 29:11 states, *"A fool uttereth all his mind: but a wise man keepeth it in till afterwards"* (KJV).

Be Acceptable in Thy Sight...

Ah, do you impart wisdom or foolishness to others? James 3:17 says, *"But the wisdom that is from above is first pure, then peaceable, gentle, and easy to be intreated, full of mercy and good fruits, without partiality, and without hypocrisy. And the fruit of righteousness is sown in peace of them that make peace"* (KJV). When we impart the wisdom of God to others, then we are acceptable to Him, for every good and every perfect gift is from above and comes down from the Father (see James 1:17). Watch what you say about others and resist the devil. Be slow to anger and always ready for reconciliation.

The Bible teaches us to be slow to anger:

> Let every man be swift to hear, slow to speak, slow to wrath: for the wrath of man worketh not the righteousness of God.
>
> —James 1:19–20 KJV

Understanding our temperament helps us to understand why we say and do certain things. Do you speak ill of others based on your past or out of arrogance? What words have you uttered today? What was the first thing you said this morning? Were you asking God's blessings for yourself and others, or were you spewing destruction all around? What was the first thing someone else said to you? What was your first conversation? Think about it. What could you do differently tomorrow?

My Strength and My Redeemer

God is a God of another chance, and every day that He blesses us on this earth is another chance to get it right. He gives us the strength to face one more day, and all it brings, through His grace and His mercy. His grace does not give us what we deserve, and His mercy gives us what we don't deserve. His grace and His mercy endure forever.

So, you say, "I'm not guilty of saying anything negative or bad about anyone else," but what did you allow to enter your spirit by listening to someone degrade and put down another person?

Let the words of my mouth, and the meditation of my heart, be acceptable in thy sight, O LORD, my strength, and my redeemer.

—Psalm 19:14 KJV

The Decisive Element

I have come to the frightening conclusion that *I* am the decisive element. It is my personal approach that creates the climate. It is my daily mood that makes the weather. I possess tremendous power to make my life miserable or joyous. I can be a tool of torture, or an instrument of inspiration. I can humiliate or humor, hurt or heal. In all situations, it is my response that decides whether a crisis will be escalated or deescalated, and a person humanized or dehumanized. If we treat people as they are, we make them worse. If we treat people as they ought to be, we help them become what they are capable of becoming.

—Johann Wolfgang von Goethe (1749–1832)

Hamm G Ginott, Apocrypha

And You Call Yourself a Christian?

While walking through the mall the other day, I came upon some items of interest. I searched for a sales associate, and to my dismay, I was met with the most unpleasant person I had recently encountered. After she looked at me as though I had leprosy, she finally asked, in a voice filled with disgust, "Can I help you?"

By then, I had an attitude myself, and I said sarcastically, "If it's not too much trouble!" Then I added, "It's not like it's your job or anything." And the battle was on. One word led to another, and we soon began to gather the attention of passersby. One such passerby was a fellow church member of mine, who was in the mall with a group of others. I spouted off a string of insults, complete with a few "non-Christian" words, then I grabbed my items and turned on my heel to find another associate. As I passed the church member who knew me, I heard her tell the others, "And she calls herself a Christian! That don't make no sense, acting like that." Honestly, as I passed her and overheard her comment, I started to lay a few choice words on her, too, but I had bigger fish to fry. She wasn't important to me at that particular point in time, so I reminded myself to deal with her and her comment later. On my heated march through the store to find another sales associate, or better yet the manager, I began to calm down. I eventually became a rational human being again, and I set the merchandise down and left the store, rationalizing to myself that I probably didn't need it anyway.

Later, I reflected upon the events of the day, and I saw how in just a split second, I had allowed myself to get angry, belittle another human being, create a scene, and act in a un-Christlike manner. I was ashamed and astounded at how things went so wrong so quickly.

Isn't it funny that there is always someone standing around waiting, lurking, just waiting to say these magic words: "And you call yourself a Christian"? No matter what the situation, there is always someone ready with a judgmental attitude, a disapproving look, someone ready to pounce with this magical phrase, as if uttering those words will change anything. Yes, I am a Christian, and yes, I miss the mark, make mistakes, lose my temper, and often put my foot in my mouth, but that doesn't make me any less of a Christian. Better yet, it proves that I am a human being, and as a human being, I'm not going to always do or say the right thing. My feelings get hurt, I occasionally get prideful, and there are times when I simply just mess up. And guess what? So do you!

Here's the beautiful revelation: God forgives me and loves me despite my mistakes, mess-ups, and everything else. All I have to do is repent and ask Him for His forgiveness. The Bible assures me that He will forgive me and cast my sins into the sea of forgetfulness, because Jesus paid the price for it all. And that's good news.

Now, I know I'm not supposed to use God's forgiveness as a crutch, or as an excuse for bad behavior. I am supposed to handle things better and be more mature than acting out, cussing someone out, or even getting physical. I also realize that there are greater consequences than someone saying, "And she calls herself a Christian," for my behavior, but still, the fact remains that I am a human being, and no, I don't always hit the mark.

Being a Christian doesn't mean that I'm going to always do and say the right thing. Being a Christian doesn't mean that I'm perfect. As a Christian, I'm a work in progress, and I'm trying to be more Christlike. A few years ago, people were wearing bracelets and T-shirts asking, "What would Jesus do?" News flash: I'm not Jesus, and yes, I fall short. My being a Christian has nothing to do with letting you or anyone else walk all over me or treat me like a doormat, either. There are no entitlements as to my letting anyone talk to me or treat me just any kind of way.

Being a Christian says that I'm supposed to pattern my life after Jesus Christ, to have His characteristics. I'm supposed to walk with the fruit of the Spirit, that is with love, joy, peace, kindness, goodness, meekness, faithfulness, and gentleness. I am to be guided by the Holy Spirit, who is my conscience and my guide. And I am to love my neighbor as myself and treat people the way I want to be treated. I am also supposed to love my enemies. Wow, that's a hard one—because it's easy to love someone who loves you in return, but it's hard to love someone who is out to cause you harm, pain, and misery. The key to all this is that as a Christian, I'm supposed to love, because Jesus is love.

Unfortunately, as a Christian, I don't always do what I'm supposed to do, nor do I act or react in a Christian way. Is this pleasing to God? Am I representing Christ to the best of my ability? The answer to these questions is a resounding no. Do I need to make changes in my

Christian walk? Yes, I do. And that requires me to understand how God has wired me. I need to understand my temperament, which is how I process and understand things. I need to understand why I do the things I do. I need to understand my shortcomings as well as my strengths. I need to know who I am, as well as whose I am. And to do this, I must examine myself. I must be honest with myself, because if I can't be honest with myself, then I can't be honest with anyone else, including God.

Someone once told me that the fourth step in the "twelve steps to sobriety" program is to write down anyone whom you're angry with, and then to write down what made you angry with that person. Finally, you must acknowledge your role in the situation or incident. The main thing in this exercise is to be honest with yourself. I found this to be quite an interesting idea—that even in the sobriety program, you must be honest with yourself. The Bible teaches us to first examine ourselves: for example, before we take communion, or before we try to pull the splinter out of our neighbor's eye without seeing the plank in our own eye. We can all fix others' problems or make suggestions as to how others should live their lives, but we rarely notice that we are doing the same things or much worse, because the rules don't apply to us. We're so busy looking over into our neighbor's yard that we can't take care of or control our own yard. There is a saying that says you should sweep around your own front door, but we can't seem to do even that, because that would require us to take a good look at our own front door. Consequently, we don't always like what we see.

When I take a good look at my front door, I see jealousy, lying, stealing, cursing, backtalk, and ditch digging, just to name a few. These are some of the flaws that I need to work on. So, what's around your front door? Moreover, for the persons who say that nothing lives around their front door, they are liars, and the truth is not in them. We all have sinned and fallen short of the glory of God, or at least that's what my Bible tells me. Our sins or flaws, if you prefer, might not be the same, but we all have them.

Here's another news flash: There's no big sin or little sin in God's eyes. There is no red sin nor blue sin; sin is sin. In addition, the Bible warns us that the wages of sin is death, but that Jesus came so that we may have life and life more abundantly (see Romans 6:23 and John 10:10). Uh-oh—hold my mule; it's shouting time right here. Most of us desire to have a life of abundance. (I say "most," because if I were to take a survey, there would undoubtedly be someone who would speak to the contrary!) What is an abundant life? It is a life that is full of love, peace, joy, and contentment. An abundant life is the life of a Christian, and it is the life that Jesus lived. It's not about money or material things, but it's about how our inside qualities are reflected in how we live our lives on the outside. I've heard it said that beauty is skin deep but ugly goes to the bone. This is an extreme example of what living a life of abundance is all about. Our inner beauty is reflected on the outside because our exterior beauty fades, but when we have ugly ways, we reflect ugliness. No amount of makeup, plastic surgery, or any of the other things we do to mask ourselves can conceal that ugliness. Ugliness is of the devil, whose sole purpose is to kill, to steal, and to destroy—and this means us. Satan wants to destroy us all, individually and collectively, but he's especially targeting our families.

So yes, I call myself a Christian—flaws, sins, and all. Jesus loves me regardless, and He gives me another chance through His goodness and mercy. He helps me to get it right every day that He extends my life. So, when you see me and I'm not quite behaving as I should, don't sound off with "And she calls herself a Christian." How about saying a little prayer that I get it right. Or maybe even greeting me or approaching me with some Christian love so that I'll stop and do better? As a Christian, when your brother falls, we're supposed to give him a helping hand up, not kick him to keep him down. That's not very Christian, and I do call myself a Christian.

Love

We are all searching for something. The overeater, the overachiever, the underachiever, the shopaholic, the shoe-aholic, the alcoholic, the chocoholic, the sexaholic, and the churchaholic—yes, I said churchaholic—are all looking for it.

What is this thing that we're all searching for in one way or another, that thing that seems so evasive and elusive? That thing that gives us the wonderful feeling of caving in to our addiction. Ah... The feeling of a new pair of shoes, that new dress, the new car, the new job, or whatever it is—that puff, that drink, or just a little more chocolate—that high we feel, or that sweet sensation that makes our toes curl, our mouth water, and our eyes glisten. That thing that, in most instances, when we realize the sad truth, is only temporary. That thing that makes us race back and forth, only to discover that we're now fixated on our next fix, which we anxiously anticipate.

Then there's the guilt and shame associated with settling for less or compromising our standards. After consuming an entire package of cookies, I shook the bag and said, "What happened to my cookies? I can't believe I ate the whole thing!" I didn't get the concept that a little will do you just fine. Now, most of us over-indulge. No one is exempt from this; it affects men, women, and children alike. Each of us is saying, "If I could just get (fill in the blank)...then I'll finally have it."

Most of us are searching for acceptance in one form or another, but all of us are captivated by the all-elusive "L" word: *love*. There, I said it.

Love, as Webster defines it, is an "intense affection for another person based on personal or familial ties." The Bible simply defines it as "God." God is love. First John 4:7–8 states it best: *"Beloved, let us love one another: for love is of God; and every one that loveth is born of God, and knoweth God. He that loveth not knoweth not God; for God is love"* (KJV). The Bible also teaches us that there are four types of love:

- *Agape*: unconditional love, Jesus' love
- *Eros*: erotic or sexual love
- *Phileo*: friendship love
- *Storge*: love for one's family

Jesus represents pure love, the love that each of us should be striving for, that love that is not based on how good we are, what we have, where we work, or how we look.

We often say, "If I can just get that job, then I can buy a new car, a new house, a new dress, and if I get lucky, I'll be able to find a good man/woman!" Oftentimes, however, instead of finding Mr. or Mrs. Right, we hook up with Mr. or Mrs. Right Now. We don't let God lead us. We end up broke, busted, and disgusted. Our egos and our self-esteem are deflated once again, and we are crying and miserable as we look to God to save us. We find ourselves playing the "could've, should've, would've" game. Weeping may endure for a night, but joy comes in the morning light (see Psalm 30:5) Then we realize that God's been there all the time. He says, *"I'll never leave you nor forsake you"* (see Hebrew 13:5). We are the ones who are chasing fading rainbows.

If we had discerned better, used better judgment, made better choices, or waited on God, we could possibly have missed making the terrible mistakes that we keep making, but isn't God wonderful? He allows us to make our own choices, even when they are the wrong choices. Ezra 7:18 states: *"And whatsoever shall seem good to thee, and to thy brethren, to do with rest of the silver and the gold, that do after the will of your God"* (KJV).

God doesn't force Himself upon us; He waits patiently for us to recognize that we need Him. Suddenly we come to the conclusion that we've tried all the rest, and now we must put God to the test.

That's when He says, "Come here, My child," with His arms open wide. In 2 Corinthians 1:3–4, the Bible states: *"Blessed be God, even the Father of our Lord Jesus Christ, the Father of mercies, and the God of all comfort; who comforteth us in all our tribulations, that we may be able to comfort them which are in any trouble, by the comfort wherewith we ourselves are comforted of God"* (KJV). He wraps His arms around us, cuddling us, protecting us, cradling us, and rocking us. Gently, ever so gently, He wipes away our tears of despair, loneliness, defeat, weakness, sadness, discontentment, and apprehension—all the things that are unlike Him.

Jesus is the very epitome of love. In John 15:9–10, Jesus declared: *"As the Father hath loved me, so have I loved you: continue ye in my love. If ye keep my commandments, ye shall abide in my love; even as I have kept my Father's commandments, and abide in his love"* (KJV). What manner of man is this, that He would give up His life for His friends? In John 10:14–15, He said, *"I am the good shepherd, and know my sheep, and am known of mine. As the Father knoweth me, even so know I the Father and I lay down my life for my sheep"* (KJV). And in John 15:12–13, He again said, *"This is my commandment, that ye love one another, as I have loved you. Greater love hath no man than this, that a man lay down his life for his friends"* (KJV). How many people are you willing to give your life up for? Most of us won't give up a bad habit, let alone our actual lives.

In John 13:36–38, Jesus said to Peter: *"Will you lay down your life for my sake? Most assuredly, I say to you, the rooster shall not crow till you have denied me three times"* (KJV). And Peter did. As soon as he denied Jesus that third time, the cock crowed and immediately Peter began to weep. In Matthew 26:75, Peter remembered the word of Jesus, and he went out and wept bitterly. The good news is that even in the midst of Peter's failure, Jesus loved him and restored him. God is a God of another chance. He says in His Word, *"A righteous man may fall seven times and rise again, but the wicked shall fall by calamity"* (Proverbs 24:16 NKJV). God restores us because of His love for us. Isn't that good news?

The Anointing

We often see people doing various things in the church like singing, preaching, and even praying, and we think, *I can do that.* Or we see the fruits of their labor, like many souls being added to the church or the establishment of a megachurch, and we say, "I could have done that." Therefore, we decide to imitate, maybe consciously or subconsciously, their actions, only to discover that although we may be able to gain a certain outcome or achieve a certain result, there is still something missing. It just isn't right.

That is the anointing.

However, often we fail to realize that anointed people are full of the Holy Spirit. First Corinthians 12:7 says, *"But the manifestation of the Spirit is given to each one for the profit of all"* (KJV). And when you are walking in the anointing, you must be dead to yourself. Romans 6:11 says we are *"to be dead indeed unto sin, but alive unto God through Jesus Christ our Lord"* (KJV). First, you have to listen to the Holy Spirit. Galatians 5:16 tells us to *"walk in the Spirit*" (KJV). And then we must die to the flesh and the flesh's desires, temptations, and pleasures. James 4:3 tells us, "*You ask and do not receive, because you ask amiss, that you may spend it on your pleasures*" (KJV).

The anointing makes all the difference in the world. We know that the anointing destroys the yoke. What exactly is the yoke? The yoke is our burdens or our bondage, the things holding us back or down. Isaiah 10:27 states, "*It shall come to pass in that day that his burden will be taken away from your shoulder, and his yoke from your neck, and the yoke will be destroyed because of the anointing oil*" (KJV).

We may practice to perfection (i.e., holy dancing, speaking in tongues ["He's coming on a Honda"]), getting the runs down right, along with all the hand gestures and movements. Or perhaps we possess charisma and a lot of pizzazz. We may even do everything we think it takes to accomplish whatever it is that we're trying to imitate, but the anointing cannot be faked. First John 2:27 states, "*But the anointing which ye have received of him abideth in you, and ye need not that any man teach you: but as the same anointing teacheth you of all things, and is truth, and is no lie, and even as it hath taught you, ye shall abideth in him*" (KJV). The anointing is not about you; it is about God speaking through you to bless others. Luke 6:19–20 tells us that "*the whole multitude sought to touch him, for power went out of him and healed them all. And he lifted up his eyes toward his disciples, and said: Blessed are ye poor, for yours is the kingdom of God"* (KJV).

The anointing is the point where God takes over and begins speaking to you. First John 2:27 tells us, *"But as the same anointing teacheth you of all thing, and is truth, and is no lie, and even as it hath taught you, you shall abide in him"* (KJV). He also moves through you, and He orders your steps.

I read somewhere that when Hollywood is preparing an actor for a specific role, the director often puts the actor into that environment, situation, or job. The actor takes notes, studies, and even videotapes the event or events. Finally, he practices and rehearses the role until the director feels satisfied that the actor has achieved the expected results. But the anointing can't be taught. The anointing comes directly from God. The Bible says in 2 Corinthians 1:21, *"Now he that establisheth us with you in Christ, and has anointed us, is God"* (KJV). It's not about you, but it is about God in you.

Through God's anointing in our lives, we are able to handle situations that would have destroyed someone else: that difficult marriage, that unmanageable child, or those fickle finances. The anointing is the Holy Spirit in that situation, and it takes authority over your situation, it lightens your burdens, and it takes away strongholds. The anointing will guide you through all of these things:

> But the anointing which you have received from him abides in you, and you do not need that anyone teach you; but as the same anointing teaches you concerning all things, and is true, and is not a lie, and just as it has taught you, you will abide in him.
>
> —1 John 2:27 KJV

While we are under the anointing, we can rejoice during our trials and tribulations. That man or woman will be saved, that child will join the church or come back to the church, and those fickle finances will pay your bills, even though you don't understand how and even though there's more month than money.

Through the anointing, our relationship with God is strengthened. This is evident in the story of the woman with the alabaster box who anointed Jesus. In Mark 14:6, Jesus told His disciples to *"leave her alone.... Why are you bothering her? She has done a beautiful thing to me"* (KJV). Then in verse 9, He said, *"Truly I tell you, wherever the gospel is preached throughout the world, what she has done will also be told, in memory of her"* (NIV). We often look at the lives of other people and we say, "They have a charmed life," or "I could have done that, if only I had been given the chance. I had the resources, if only they had believed in me..." Why do they have what they have? It's because they are anointed with that life. As 1 John 2:20 states, *"You have an anointing from the Holy One and you know all things"* (KJV).

I heard a preacher once say during his sermon that for a number of years he pastored a church that he had to drive several hours to get to for the Sunday morning service and the Wednesday night Bible study. He only had a few members, but that didn't matter. He diligently made the trip every week. But one day, after many years of this, he just couldn't do it anymore. What had changed? He was the same man, the same preacher, pastoring the same church, making the same drive—the same everything. What changed was the anointing. It was time to go, time to move on. When God tells us to go, then we must go. Ecclesiastes 3:1 teaches us that for everything there is a season and a time to every purpose under heaven.

We sing the words of a well-known chorus: "where He leads me, I will follow," but the anointing is the difference between just going and going. Jonah was anointed to go to Nineveh, but he felt he knew better than God and he decided to go to down to Tarshish instead.

> *Now the word of the LORD came to Jonah the son of Amittai, saying, "Arise, go to Nineveh, that great city, and cry out against it; for their wickedness has come up before Me." But Jonah arose to flee to Tarshish from the presence of the LORD. He went down to Joppa, and found a ship going to Tarshish; so he paid the fare, and went down into it, to go with them to Tarshish from the presence of the LORD.*
>
> —Jonah 1:1–3 NKJV

Without the anointing, we can do nothing. Have you ever wondered why someone with a voice that is all over the scales can reach your spirit and stir up your emotions, but someone who sings perfectly, hitting each note with perfection, can leave you cold and empty inside? It's the anointing. I've said it and heard it said on many occasions: "Many are called, but few are chosen." One lady added the phrase, "And some just went." So, ask yourself, if many are called (who's doing the calling?) and few are chosen (by God), then where do the others come in? Some just went (by whose authority?).

We may say, "I can do that"; "If (so and so) can, then I *know* I can"; or "I'm just as saved as they are, and probably more because I—" That's when the "me, myself, and I complex" jumps in. We all know that the anointing destroys the yoke. John 8:36 says, *"Therefore if the Son makes you free, you shall be free indeed"* (KJV).

Songs have been sung about it, preachers have preached about it, but exactly what is the anointing? I searched the dictionary, and not even Mr. Webster could define it, because he didn't understand it. I searched *Nelson's Illustrated Bible Dictionary*, and it said, "To authorize or set apart a person for a particular work or service." The New Testament refers to the anointing of the Holy Spirit, which brings understanding, and it is for everyone who believes in Jesus Christ. The dictionary goes on to say that it can occur physically, as in "anoint my head with oil," or spiritually, as the Holy Spirit anoints a person's heart and mind with the love and truth of God. I've heard preachers say that the anointing means "to smear on." However, I have concluded that the anointing involves aligning yourself with God's purpose for your life. It is the presence of God through the Holy Spirit. Acts 10:38 speaks of *"how God anointed Jesus of Nazareth with the Holy Ghost and with power, who went about doing good and healing all who were oppressed by the devil, for God was with Him"* (NKJV). And we can say along with Paul, who wrote these words in Philippians 4:13: *"I can do all things through Christ who strengthens me"* (NKJV). The Bible also says in Jeremiah

20:9, *"His word was in my heart like a burning fire shut up in my bones"* (NKJV).

When the anointing is in your life, people don't act the same way around you that they used to. Second Samuel 22:51 states: *"He is the tower of salvation to His king, and shows mercy to His anointed, to David and his descendants forevermore"* (NKJV). They don't treat you the same way. It's not something you can control. You don't have to loudly shout to be seen or heard. Ephesians 2:10 tells us, *"For we are His workmanship, created in Christ Jesus for good works, which God prepared beforehand ordained that we should walk in them"* (NKJV). As we walk in the anointing of God, we go where God wills, do what God wills, and say what God wills. Actually, it's nothing that you do; it relates to your mere presence. The devil recognizes God in you and trembles (see James 2:19). When the anointing is on your life, people won't ask you to do dumb things; on the contrary, they will try to be around you in order to be blessed. Anointed people are full of the Holy Spirit, and people are then attracted to them. Lots of times this becomes a trap or a trick of the devil, because people tend to worship them and make idols out of them. Please beware of this, because God doesn't share His glory with anyone. On the contrary, God is a jealous God.

When you are anointed, there's something different about you. You radiate an aura or a glow. When you speak, it's with wisdom. As Ecclesiastes 2:26 declares, *"God giveth to a man that is good in his sight wisdom, and knowledge and joy..."* (KJV). Everything you do is to the glory of God, just as 1 Corinthians 10:31 states: *"Whether therefore you eat, or drink, or whatsoever ye do, do all to the glory of God"* (KJV). Your "self" is totally removed. Your witness is not forced or faked; on the contrary, it's real—so real that souls are edified, spirits are lifted, and your witness is stronger. Lives are delivered. The Bible instructs us to present our bodies as a living sacrifice, holy and acceptable unto God (see Romans 12:1).

God can anoint you in the presence of other people. I've often heard preachers say, "I'm waiting for my help." Simply put, they are waiting for God to give them utterance. Under the anointing, "the Word" flows, and without the anointing, "the Word" won't flow. And God will anoint you in spite of other people. Those folks who put you down, who talked about you, and who waited for you to fail, they are ditch-diggers, liars, and just plain chimps. Yes, *chimps* not *chumps*. Chumps at least work toward something; chimps are there simply to entertain. People have to be willing to receive the anointing from the person whom God is sending it through.

If they don't want to receive it, the Bible instructs us to shake the dust from our feet:

> "If the household is worthy, let your peace come it. But if it is not worthy, let your peace return to you. And whoever will not receive you nor hear your words, when you depart from that house or city, shake off the dust from your feet."
> —Matthew 10:13–14 NKJV

Always remember it's not you, but Christ who lives inside of you, that gives you the anointing. Everyone in your inner circle should be walking with God, and if they are not, then you cannot have them in your life or your inner circle. Everyone in your inner circle must be aligned with God's purpose for their lives; remember, the anointing is God's purpose for your life.

With the anointing, you're not shy anymore; you sing or speak with holy boldness. Acts 4:31 tells us what happened to the early disciples: *"And when they had prayed, the place where they were assembled together was shaken; and they were all filled with the Holy Spirit, and they spoke the word of God with boldness"* (NKJV). We can receive His power: (Is40:29 *"He gives power to the weak, and to those who have no might He increases strength"* (Isaiah 40:29 NKJV). And in Acts 1:8, Jesus said: *"But you shall* receive power when the Holy Spirit has come upon you, and you shall be witnesses to Me in Jerusalem, and in all Judea and Samaria, and to the end of the earth" (NKJV). We must enthusiastically strive to be in His will (see Jesus' prayer in Matthew 6:10). You forget about yourself, and all your cares and fears are removed. With the anointing, it's all about forgiveness, deliverance, and redemption. The anointing adds quality and satisfaction to your life. God accomplishes these things in you through and with His anointing. The Bible instructs us to "seek first the kingdom of God" (Matthew 6:33 NKJV); simply put, if we seek God above all else, He will give us everything we need and even some of our wants. Hebrews 11:6 tell us that "without faith it is impossible to please Him for he who comes to God must believe that He is, and that He is a rewarder of those who diligently seek Him" (NKJV).

Church Folk

We might expect resistance and criticism from the Sadducees (the priests) and the Pharisees (the lawyers)—but *the apostles?* The apostles had been chosen by Jesus, and they walked, talked, slept, and ate with Him. They experienced Him firsthand. They experienced His unconditional love, His forgiveness, and His power. They witnessed His miracles, along with His death, burial, and resurrection, and yet they still questioned Him. The apostles were "church folk."

"Church folk" embodies three types of people. First, church folk can be natural people; these individuals are only interested in material things, the here and the now. They have an "if it feels good or looks good to me, it must be for me" mentality, and they seek to satisfy their fleshly desires and craving. The second type are the spiritual ones; these individuals have the mind of Christ. They have put away childish things. They are no longer doing the same things they used to do, nor are they going the same places they used to go. They have

given up things for the Lord. Moreover, they have out-
grown some things. Finally, there are the carnal folks;
these individuals straddle the fence. These folks are not
natural all the time, nor are they spiritual all the time.
They have issues.

What's up with "church folk"? Have you noticed that
your greatest criticisms come from church folk? The
good folk, the *ecclesia*—the called out, sanctified, filled
with the Holy Ghost, Bible-toting, speaking in tongues
(but *whose* tongues?)—spiritual folk are the ones to
judge us more quickly and harshly.

I ask "whose tongues" because some of the things
that come out of their mouths are definitely not of God.
For instance, a young lady once told me when we were
talking about all the ministers we work with, that ministers are nothing but undercover pimps. Then she confessed that she was a Christian!

Some church folk spew more harm, hurt, and damage than anyone else, and they do it all in the name of
Jesus. Some church folk can and will kill you spiritually—and sometimes physically. They kill you spiritually
by causing many to backslide or leave the church alto-
gether. And they can kill you physically, causing physical harm or death. One example of this is when Cain
killed Abel (see Genesis 4:8). When a person falls or fal-
ters, we are supposed to help them get back up, encour-

age them, and pray for them, not condemn then, talk about them, and criticize them. We sit around giving them the side-eye, making snide comments and rejecting them, trying to run them out of church.

Recently, I had the privilege to speak with an older gentleman (we'll call him Tom) who confessed that he hadn't always been saved. He told me that in his heyday, he used to love the fruit of the vine. He said that, thanks to a deacon who kept coming around and checking on him, he was saved today. He said he told that deacon to quit wasting his time 'cause he wasn't ready yet, but every so often the deacon would show up to check on him. I smiled as he continued his story. He then told me that he went to church—not the one that the deacon attended, but a different church. He said he was already self-conscious about being there and was feeling a bit uneasy. However, he began to feel better after overhearing a conversation between one of the "good" church folk (we'll call her Bea) and another gentleman who partook of the vine (we'll call him Willie). Moreover, the conversation went something like this: Bea, the church folk, asked Willie (a well-known drunk who was seated behind her), "What are you doing in church?" Willie, not missing a beat, replied, "The same as you. What are you doing here?" After that conversation, Tom said he began to relax, and he realized he had just as much right to be there as anyone else. Bea had an unsavory reputation herself, and while she was questioning Willie, she forgot that people knew her skeletons too. Afterward, Bea turned around and shut her mouth. I applauded the deacon, Willie, and Tom. My pastor says that we should let get them in the back door, and then move them to the sanctuary where they can learn about the love of Jesus Christ. Jesus said, *"I...will draw all men unto me"* (John 12:32 KJV). How can Jesus draw them if we won't even give Him a chance and stay out of His way? We keep running people away instead of welcoming them in.

Have you noticed that if a person doesn't look or act a certain way, some church folk have no problem running them away, instead of embracing them with the love of the Lord. The Bible says we have all sinned and fallen short of the glory of God (see Romans 3:23), so who do you think you are? Surely not God, that you can stand in judgment of your brother. So, the looming question is, how can you say, "I love God," whom you have not seen, and hate your brother, whom you see every day?

As a child, I was taught the life lesson that "if you can't say something nice, then don't say anything at all." However, this rule doesn't seem to apply to some church folk. Not only will they say things to you, but they also talk about you behind your back. And they don't even have to know you or know that what they are saying is true. And nowhere in my life lesson did it say to lie; it said to not say anything at all. There is a big, big difference between saying nothing and lying.

In addition, what I find to be extremely funny is that the same people who will lie just to have something to talk about, are the same ones who will lose their minds when the tables are turned and the lie is about them. Someone once said, "Great minds talk about ideas, average minds talk about the events, and small minds talk about people." *Wow!* Unfortunately, the author is unknown, because there has never been a more accurate sentence.

Churches are supposed to be the hospital for the hurting, the addicted, and the lost, but because of some church folk, people aren't being delivered, healed, or saved. Jesus said in Matthew 9:12, *"It is not the healthy who need a doctor, but the sick"* (NIV). Once some church folks make up their minds about something, that's the way it is. No matter how much good you've done or are doing, nothing will change their preconceived notions about you. They stand in judgment based solely on their ideology, without all the facts. I was taught that there are two sides to every story, and there's a lot of information that you are not privy to; in other words, there are always things you don't know. You don't know, and you weren't there, but sister or brother so-and-so said it, so it has to be true. And they run with it.

The sad truth of the matter is that usually the situation, story, or whatever has nothing to do with us. It doesn't add to or take away from our lives or our spirituality. Most of the time, the situation is personal. It's between God and that person or persons. Although it has nothing to do with us as people, we make it our business. We just have to have something to talk about. People often talk just to hear themselves talk.

When God is using you, some church folks will try to shut you down and sabotage your blessing. Some church folks can be some of the most negative people in the world. When you are using your spiritual gifts to do what God has asked you to do, here comes the church folk, the naysayers. Their sole mission is to stop whatever it is that God has assigned you to do, by any means necessary. Some of them seek merely to discourage you; others seek to stop you dead in your tracks. When God called me to become a deacon, I kept it to myself. I told people only when it was absolutely necessary, and then it was only because I had a class to go to while I was in training. I wasn't specific; I only said that I had a class to attend at church. The closer it came to ordination; I began telling a few people, and only a few, that I was being ordained and when. After some time during my training, however, people began to see me serving communion, walking the aisle, etc. A so-called friend, the spokesman for the church folk, told me that I could never serve her communion because I would sweat in the juice. Not only did she make this horrible statement to me, but she said it in front of a group of people, and they all laughed. It made me even more self-conscious than I had been before. When I get nervous, I sweat, and I've always had a fear of tripping and spilling the communion wine all over everyone's clothes, dropping the trays, or falling and rolling down the aisle—and worst-case scenario, all three happening simultaneously. How many people are not doing what God has called them to do because of church folk?

Not only do some church folks hurt you with their mouths, but they also tend to think they are entitled. Don't you dare sit in their seat, or park in their parking space. All hell will break loose, and you've got to go. On one occasion, I visited a church during a revival. I got there early and chose a seat near the front. A lady came to the pew where I was sitting and stood there. I greeted her with a smile and continued reading my Bible, attempting to meditate before the service started. She cleared her throat, then looked at me as if to tell me to move. I again smiled. Then she proudly announced that I was sitting in her seat. I politely moved over, but unfortunately then I was in someone else's seat, which created the same problem. At that point, I thought, *Is this the way you treat guests?* This was the first time I'd ever visited this church. Needless to say, I've never been back to that particular church.

If these church folks ever thought about how others see them, most would shudder in disbelief. How you treat people will affect the entire service. No one wants to be in a service where they feel unwanted or inferior. It's not always what we say that offends others; it could be our body language as well. I went to Bible study one night, and before the study, the church had a prayer meeting. The question was asked by the leader, "Who experienced God today?" After someone else gave their testimony, I stood up and was relating what I had experienced that day. The leader of the Bible study looked at me as though I was dirt, then she rolled her eyes and turned her head. Since I'm not a babe in Christ, I continued giving my testimony and detailing my experience. I didn't allow her attitude to discourage me. The wonderful ending to the story was when the minister got up to preach her sermon and she affirmed my testimony.

But still: I'd like to examine this. What if I had been a babe in Christ? Would I have sat down and not shared my testimony, and then lost a wonderful opportunity to share the love of Jesus Christ? Others would not have been encouraged by my testimony. Would I have left church vowing never to return? Would I have called her out? Or would I have walked up and punched her in the face for disrespecting me? I could have reacted in so many ways, as do other people who have been offended at church. The leader came off as arrogant, snobbish, and disrespectful. Did she mean to? I don't know but look at the damage that could have been done. Since I was offended, let's face it: I definitely would have told others of my experience, and I would have told them that they wouldn't be welcome at that church, and that they should not attend. Here's a question to ponder: Is that the kind of message we want to convey about the church and the people within it? Jesus talked to everyone, from the gutter-most to the uttermost. No one was too lowly, and no one was too high or esteemed for Jesus to take the time to speak with them. As a matter of fact, Jesus hung out with the outcast of society (see Matthew 9:11–12).

Does your church represent Jesus or something else? And if your answer was "something else," what is it?

Isn't it funny how some church folk can find a scripture to justify how badly they treat you? History teaches us that slave masters and owners—all of whom confessed to be Christians—used the Word of God to condone their mistreatment of slaves. And yet today we're still doing the same thing. We're quick to say, "The Bible says this and that." We make the Bible say whatever it is we want to have justified, but God had this to say in Revelation 22:18–19 (NKJV):

> *For I testify to everyone who hears the words of the prophecy of this book: If anyone adds to these things, God will add to him the plagues that are written in this book; and if anyone takes away from the words of the book of this prophecy, God shall take away his part from the Book of Life, from the holy city, and from the things which are written in this book.*

...that we shall neither add to nor take away from the words of the Book. Jesus came that we might have life and life more abundantly (see John 10:10). But if it was left up to church folks, that wouldn't be a possibility.

Thank God for His amazing grace! Without God's grace, we would all be in trouble. Gods' grace is given to us freely. We didn't do anything to earn it, and we can't solicit it. We don't deserve it, it's unwarranted, and we can't do anything to gain it. It's given to us because of God's love and generosity. God is the only One who can make us right (see Hosea 14:9), and He didn't wait for us to get ourselves right before coming to save us. We can't save ourselves; we need God. Jesus is the way, the truth, and the life (see John 14:6). Isn't it wonderful that God's grace is so amazing? Despite some church folks, He still blesses us and keeps us.

It was the "church folk" who sought judgment against Jesus. It was the "church folk" who beat our Lord and Savior and nailed Him to the cross. And when He asked for something to drink, they gave him vinegar instead of water. It was "church folk" who crucified our Lord on Golgotha that Friday. It was "church folk" who sealed the opening to the tomb, trying to keep Him in the grave. The good news is that even death couldn't keep Him, and on that third day, He got up from the grave, for you and for me, and for those good ol' "church folk" too.

Humility

I know a man who constantly tries to make everyone around him feel inadequate, insignificant, and inferior. His arrogance is proudly flaunted so that no one is aware that he himself actually feels underappreciated, insignificant, and invaluable. How arrogant for him to act as if he is so fabulous that the world would totally fall apart without him.

The Bible warns us to not think of ourselves more highly than we ought (see Romans 12:3). But somewhere along the line, a few folks missed it. Whether accidental or on purpose, we have a real problem. What's the problem? you may ask. The problem is people who are arrogant. I'm not implying that you cannot have and exhibit self-confidence. By all means, have confidence, but there's a difference between confidence and arrogance. The Bible teaches us in three separate scriptures to be humble:

Be completely humble and gentle.
> —Ephesians 4:2 NIV

Humble yourselves before the Lord.
> —James 4:10 NIV

Humble yourselves, therefore, under God's mighty hand.
> —1 Peter 5:6

So, if the Bible is encouraging us to be humble, then exactly what does it mean to be humble? *Humility* is defined as "being humble; without false pride, arrogance, and vanity." The attitude of the Christian should be to not think more highly of himself than he ought to think, but to have sound judgment, according to Romans 12:3. It is knowing our true position before God. It is not self-abasement or the demeaning of one's self. So, for the purpose of our current conversation, we will define *humility* as "the Christian attitude of not being vain, of being free from excessive pride and arrogance, and to think using sound judgment." This definition sounds good to me.

Let's explore this a bit. We must first truly define what *confidence* and *arrogance* are before we can distinguish between the two. *Confidence* is defined as "a belief in yourself and your abilities." *Arrogance* is defined as "a feeling of superiority above and over everyone else." [1]

Therefore, by using our definition of humility, we can see that there is no room for arrogance in our lives. The Bible says that none of us has the right to brag or boast about anything (see Proverbs 27:1–2).

Don't be fooled—you are not "all that." And the world doesn't revolve around you. Stop thinking that it does. You may be in good health today; you may have a house on the hill, a "good" job, and a little money in the bank; you may be living high on the hog. In a split second, it could all collapse around you. Know this and know this well: In a split second, your life could change drastically. The loss of a job, a family crisis, a medical emergency, or some other catastrophic situation could lead to financial hardship; it doesn't and wouldn't take much. There are families sleeping in cars that once had it all. Remember, your success is not based on what you have, on material things; it's on how you use what you have been given.

We have no right to look down on anyone, no matter how insignificant we think they are. That person whom you think is insignificant may be just the person you need in a crisis. The Bible says in Matthew 20:16, *"And the last shall be first and the first shall be last"* (KJV). Who do <u>you</u> think you are, looking down your nose at

1 From yourdictionary.com.

anyone? This includes the person who is down on their luck, the person who doesn't look or smell like you think they should. You are still no better than they are. Remember, at any given time that person just might be you or someone you care about. There are chronic alcoholics, prostitutes, drug dealers, and addicts with more class in their little fingers than some of us who think we are so much. Therefore, be humble. And don't try and fake it to make it, either. Be genuine. Keep it real! God knows and other people can tell when you're being fake and phony. Although you can fool people, you can never fool God. False humility is just as bad as no humility at all.

Self-confidence is truly a remarkable and outstanding personality trait to have. I even can accept it if it is bordering on arrogance, but don't cross the line. Once you cross the line from self-confidence to arrogance, you have a real problem. It becomes a real turnoff, a character flaw. Arrogance divides you from you. It also divides you from people who would otherwise be there for you to help you.

There is nothing wrong with having pride. We're supposed to have pride: pride in ourselves, pride in our children and families, pride in our work, pride in our churches, and pride in our homes. There's nothing wrong with pride as long as it doesn't become all-consuming. According to Proverbs 16:18–19, *"Pride goes before destruction, and a haughty spirit before a fall. Better to be of a humble spirit with the lowly, than to be divide the spoil with the proud"* (KJV). We should not take pride in the wrong things, such as saying, "My child is a gang banger," or "My child is a drug dealer." Where is the pride in that?

I'm a parent, and I'm proud of my children and their accomplishments, but I don't go around throwing their successes and accomplishments in other people's faces or looking down on others because their children haven't accomplished the same things as mine have. I also don't believe that everyone is jealous of my children or that anyone's child is less than my children. I consider my children blessed, and I feel blessed that God has allowed my children to succeed. I also try to assist or encourage other children along the way, not comparing them to my children, but helping them to find their own successes and accomplishments. I fully understand that each child is different, and they are all capable of success. At my house, we practice excellence and not perfection. Excellence is being the best you that you can be. And that's healthy pride.

Arrogance, on the other hand, is my telling another parent whose child may have dropped out of school that their child would never be anything, have anything, or accomplish anything other than going to jail, or worse, being killed. That is arrogance and foolish pride, along with ignorance, trying to compare children by setting the standards based solely on their own children. Second Corinthians 10:12 states: *"For we dare not close ourselves with those who commend themselves. But they, measuring themselves by themselves, and comparing themselves among themselves, are not wise"* (KJV). This verse warns us against that very thing. The Bible also warns in James 4:6: *"But he giveth more grace. Wherefore he saith, God resisteth the proud, but giveth grace to the humble"* (KJV). Oops, there's that word humble again.

We must learn to look at ourselves honestly. Galatians 6:3 tells us: *"For if a man think himself to be something, when he is nothing, he deceiveth himself"* (KJV). And we must not exhibit foolish pride. We are to walk as we live, and that is in the Spirit, without vanity (see Galatians 5:25–26). Luke 10:20 tells us that *"we should rejoice, because your names are written in heaven, not in the power, spiritual gifts, and talents that He gives"* (NKJV). It's not about you, but it's about the love, power, grace, and mercy of God.

When God Speaks

On a blistering hot August day, while I was walking to school to retrieve my grandson, I began to notice the drying creek bed, the sun-scorched grass, and the patches of dirt where grass used to be along my path. I wondered why I had chosen to walk instead of drive my car so I would be in the cool air-conditioning—had I lost my mind? According to the weather reports, we were in the midst of a drought. Officials had already placed restrictions on grass watering and car washing. Suddenly, I noticed some beautiful wildflowers growing in the midst of all the dryness. I began to praise God. Why? Because in that instant He began to speak to me, saying that He was present even in the desert places. When all around me was death and destruction, here were these beautiful purple and yellow flowers, growing where nothing else could grow.

Have you ever wondered when you're praying if God hears you? Moreover, if He is listening, what is He thinking and what does He have to say? The Bible says that God spoke in various ways such as through dreams, people, images, prophecies, angels, direct commands, and visions. However, that was back then, and it was written to those individuals. What about now—does God still speak? More importantly, does God speak to us?

God is speaking all the time. The problem is that we may be too busy to heed what He has to say. Most of us don't realize that these are not the only ways that God speaks to us. God speaks to us based on our own personal relationship with Him. He meets us where we are in our relationship with Him. With all that we go through, just trying to live our lives, does God have anything to say to us?

Has God spoken to you? I believe He's speaking to us—perhaps we're not listening or He's not saying what we want to hear. When God speaks, He doesn't need any help from us. We shouldn't try to fit Him into a box and limit His voice. We simply need to take the time and just listen to Him.

How and when does God speak to us? Well, I'm glad you asked. He speaks as we live, work, and play, from day to day. While we are driving down the road and listening to our favorite radio station, the DJ may say something or play a song that resonates in our spirit. Perhaps suddenly a billboard catches our eye, and there's a message there just for us. God can use a commercial or a bumper sticker as a subtle reminder, quickening our spirit. Have you ever had to pull over and just cry or rejoice because the presence of the Lord was all around you?

Perhaps we get to work, and in the elevator, He uses other people or the elevator music itself. Alternatively, while we are walking past a bulletin board, something may jump out at us, sending our soul leaping for joy, or breaking us down like a crying baby. There could also be an e-mail or a memo in our morning messages. Perhaps He speaks through a phone call that might have started out unpleasant but then God steps in.

How about a song that keeps playing repeatedly in the recesses of your mind and you just cannot make it go away, no matter how hard you try, then suddenly you feel compelled to sing it out loud and clear? Maybe you are in a store shopping and a familiar sound or smell strikes a warm memory of your grandmother, mother, or someone else who has prayed for you, and/or you find yourself singing and giving praise and honor to God?

God is not limited as to how He speaks, and He can speak to us anywhere, at any time, by any means; maybe He will speak to us while we are banking, reading a book, walking, or at our child's daycare or school. Possibly that person who is passing by could be the individual whom God uses to bless or to be blessed by us. Be careful how you treat the people around you because the Word says you may be entertaining angels unaware (see Hebrews 13:2), so that person may just be what God ordered.

God is so wonderfully awesome. He can speak to us through the television, through a child, a flower, a sunset or sunrise, snow and ice, desert places, a picture, or a gentle breeze across your face. Maybe He will speak while we are working in the yard or doing that job we just hate to do—like ironing or washing the dishes. Personally, I hate to iron, but when God is speaking to me sometimes He reminds me that I'm just like that article of clothing. He has to press the wrinkles out of my life, and if I'm stubborn, He has to add a little steam and some starch. On the other hand, like when I am washing the dishes, He reminds me that He needs to dip me a couple of times and even scrape off some of the crap to make me clean and shining like new. Everyone wants to eat off the shiny new plate, not one that has food stuck on it and is nasty and dirty. That's God—He will make us clean on the inside, and that will be reflected on the outside as we are shiny and new. The Bible says, *"Therefore if any man be in Christ, he is a new creature: old things are passed away; behold, all things are become new"*

(2 Corinthians 5:17 KJV). Even while we are working on a crossword puzzle, we may see the word "is" and suddenly start reflecting on who God is... Hallelujah!

You see, God doesn't have to shout really loud, because He can use the simple and the little things in life to speak to us and through us. We just have to be willing to listen to Him and take notice. Something as simple as when we find a penny—that's God. You may ask how finding a penny can be God. It's because every time we look at that penny, it says, "In God we trust." That is good news! We should all be trusting God, not man, not our jobs, not the president, but God (see Hebrews 12:2). All of the other things can fail, but not God. God can do anything but fail. Moreover, the Word says that heaven and earth will pass away before one jot of His Word fails (see Matthew 24:35). Every day we should ask God to speak to us and to give us an ear to hear His voice.

There are endless possibilities as to the ways God chooses to speak to us; unfortunately, we are so busy we cannot always hear Him speak or we do not take the time to be obedient. We miss the opportunity to speak or spread the good news of Jesus Christ.

God has given us technological advancements so that He will get the glory and the praise. A prime example is the telephone. Today we can share the goodness of God and His gentle mercies through our conversations, shared photos, and text messages. The Bible warns us to let our conversations be holy, so we need to watch what we say and what we share. Ah, the marvels of God! God made everything for His glory.

Here's the truly amazing revelation: God uses my thoughts, my pains, and my writing to bless me as well as others. These examples show that God is omnipresent, omniscient, and omni-sneaky! God once used a friend to tell me that this message was not finished. I would like thank God for using my friend, and I thank my friend for allowing God to use them to speak to me. God uses unsuspecting situations and people to speak to each of us.

There are times when God speaks through another person and the individual doesn't even know that he or she has said something to bless and/or minister to us. That's just how God works—when He has a message for you, it's for you, and if you're listening or looking for it, you'll receive it. God started me writing, and I really didn't think I had anything to say, but He has given me the words to say. God has blessed me so much, because each time I read over what I've written He gives me new insights and new messages.

God even speaks through death. None of us likes to have to go through the experience of losing a loved one, but the truth of the matter is that some of us would never look to God if it were not for death. Sometimes God has to remove some people from our lives so that He can get our attention. On the other hand, there are times when He adds people to our lives, if only for a season or a reason, to get our attention as well. In both instances, God can use death to accomplish this goal.

God can use our situations or life crises to speak to us also. If we never had a problem, how would we know that God could solve them? We all are in the middle of a situation, just come out of a situation, or are going into a situation, and God will speak to us through these rough and troubling times. Remember that God spoke to Abraham (see Genesis 17:1); Jacob dreamed dreams (see Genesis 28:12); Joseph interpreted dreams (see Genesis 40:9); and Saul prophesied (see 1 Samuel 10:10). God uses ordinary people to do extraordinary things by simple means. He'll raise up people to do His will. God used Mary, a virgin girl, to give birth to our Lord and Savior, Jesus Christ. Jesus was a carpenter by trade, but He gave up His life for the remission of our sins. He was buried in a borrowed tomb, and early on the third morning, He rose from the grave with all power in His hands.

Peace

The peace that passes all understanding embodies more than just the peace of spirituality. It is inclusive of emotional, physical, and financial well-being, as well. It is the kind of peace that can only come from God through the Holy Spirit. Romans 5:1 says this: *Therefore being justified by faith, we have peace with God through our Lord Jesus Christ"* (KJV). What kind of peace is this? I'm referring to *shalom*.

In searching for a greater understanding of *shalom*, I discovered that I had to begin by inquiring as to the definition of *peace*. I traveled through the *Nelson's Bible Dictionary*, and through my concordance, but to my dismay, I didn't quite find a definitive definition of this word. However, I did find several reference points, as follows: The Old Testament meaning of *peace* was "the completeness, soundness, and well-being of the total person" (per Wikipedia). This peace is God-given, and it is only obtained as a gift from God. Ephesians 2:8 states, *"For by grace are ye saved through faith; and that not*

of yourselves: it is the gift of God" (KJV). Peace also has a
physical meaning, as in Psalm 4:8: *"I will both lie down
in peace, and sleep; for You alone, O LORD, make me dwell
in safety"* (NKJV). It has the mental health component
of contentment, as in Isaiah 26:3: *"You will keep him in
perfect peace, whose mind is stayed on You, because he trusts
in You"* (NKJV). It has the financial aspect of prosperity,
as in Psalm 122:6–7: *"Pray for the peace of Jerusalem: May
they prosper who love you. May peace be within your walls,
and prosperity within your palaces"* (NKJV). And it has
the meaning of the absence of war, as in 1 Samuel 7:14:
*"Then the cities which the Philistines had taken from Israel
were restored to Israel, from Ekron to Gath; and Israel recov-
ered its territory from the hands of the Philistines. Also there
was peace between Israel and the Amorites"* (NKJV).

In the New Testament, *peace* refers to the inner tranquility and poise of the Christian whose trust in God
comes through Christ. The peace that Jesus spoke of
during His Sermon on the Mount was a combination
of hope, trust, and quiet in the mind and soul, brought
about by reconciliation with God (see Matthew 5:9).

And then I was guided to the source, the Bible itself,
by the Holy Spirit, and I found what I had been seeking:
the definition of *peace*. The Bible defines peace this way:
*"The peace of God, which passeth all understanding, shall keep
your hearts and minds through Christ Jesus"* (Philippians

4:7 KJV). This, to me, means we are given a peace that doesn't make sense. To me this says that Jesus will guard my heart and mind and that He'll give me peace. The peace of God—now that's good news.

Through Jesus we experience peace, because He'll give you peace in the midst of your storm (see Mark 4:39). This peace is as soft as a gentle breeze moving across a blanket of sun-drenched flowers in a cool meadow on a warm spring day. It is as pure as the freshly falling snow that drifts slowly down like clouds floating down to blanket the cool earth during the crisp winter months. And it is as deliberate as each snowflake, formed in exactly the same way, that will cover the earth, but when examined individually, will maintain its own distinctive identity, characteristics, and beauty—for science has taught us that no two snowflakes are exactly alike. They are individually and wonderfully made. This peace is as spontaneous as a summer shower that appears suddenly, dropping just enough rain to take the steam out of a scorching day, but then stops just in time to let the festivities continue.

God is *mag-tab-ulous* enough to grant you perfect peace, the peace that no other person can supply or grant. It is the peace that calms all your fears and dries all your tears, that takes the pain away and pulls the sting out of death. I'm searching for that peace.

God has called us to peace (see 1 Corinthians 7:15). The Bible instructs us to strive for peace with everyone (see Hebrews 12:14). That person with whom you had that argument and you just can't seem to let it go? Do just that—let it go.

The Bible teaches us that when we have a problem with our brother or sister, we are to go to them. If the matter is still not settled, we are to take another person with us as a mediator and go back to that one. If the matter is still not settled, then we are to take the matter before the church. (see Matthew 18:15). In most cases, the matter can be settled the first time, because most problems are generally matters of miscommunication. The Bible further instructs us to live peaceably with all in Romans 12:18: *"If it be possible, as much as lieth in you, live peaceably with all men"* (KJV), and to live a peaceful life in our homes and neighborhoods (see Isaiah 32:18). We are to have a quiet life, as is stated in 1 Timothy 2:2: We are to pray *"for kings, and for all that are in authority; that we may lead a quiet and peaceable life in all godliness and honesty"* (KJV). In order to live peaceably with everyone, some things we have to settle, but others we just have to walk away from. We also need to mind our own business and quit worrying about what the neighbors are doing. We need to quit trying to keep up with everybody else. We should be doing what is required of us.

So how will you know when you have obtained this kind of peace? What are the results of peace? I'm glad you asked. First, there will be nothing missing and nothing broken. Your life will not always be in an uproar. Your life will be complete, with nothing missing. Your finances and your family will be at harmony, with nothing broken. Secondly, your actions will change, and you'll develop a level of calmness equal to those of Gandhi and Mother Teresa. You won't speak in their vernacular, but you will have that feeling of serenity and calmness. Thirdly, you'll have more compassion, more patience, and most of all, more love. We often quote Proverbs 15:1: *"A soft answer turns away wrath"* (KJV), that is, our ability to look beyond the person's anger and see deep into their heart to find their need, that is what will bring peace to a situation. Oftentimes we are so busy looking on the outside that we miss what's going on on the inside. God doesn't. He looks at the heart. Love penetrates. And God is love. Love covers a multitude of sins. That's shouting news right there—because of God's love, we can and we must go on. Only through God's love can we obtain peace. And finally, as you begin seeking God, you will become enlightened from the natural into the spiritual, for the Bible says, *"In all [our] ways acknowledge him, and he shall direct [our] paths"* (Proverbs 3:6 KJV). The Beatitudes become a guiding influence in your life: *"Blessed are the peacemakers: for they shall be called the children of God"* (Matthew 5:9 KJV). Peace happens from the inside out.

The Bible mentions seven people in the Old Testament as ones who were peaceful. Isn't that something? To be recorded in the Bible as "peaceful"—now, that's an accomplishment. For some of us, the only time we're mentioned anywhere is for being hellraisers, for being difficult and acting a fool. All of us want to be remembered, but for what exactly? Sit down and try to think of how you would like to be remembered. Personally, I'd like to be remembered as fearing God, loving life, and making a positive difference in the lives of others. I don't want to be remembered for all the things I've done wrong or what I didn't accomplish—unless it helps someone else along their journey. I want my mistakes to shine the light on the correct way of achieving accomplishments and doing things, and for my failures to lead to someone else's greatest successes.

If you were to die today, what would people say about you? If you could be a fly on the wall, what would you hear about yourself? Would people say, "Run, she is nothing but trouble"? Would they call you a gossip, or a liar? How about a thief or a cheat? What would your friends and loved ones say? If we have peace and tranquility in our lives, we don't have to give this a second thought. Why? Because with peace in our lives, we aren't rowdy. Gossip doesn't interest us and lying won't be a part of us. Several people have sent me text messages that said, "Be honest and tell me what you think about me." Well, with the persons who sent that text to me, I lost a few relationships—because I was honest! We ask people to be honest, but honesty is not always what we're seeking. We actually are seeking flattery, praises, and accolades.

A person I once dated pointed out that I always asked open-ended and loaded questions. I thought, *I do not!* and I acted appalled. However, I began to pay attention and I discovered that I really do. I ask questions that will lead people to tell me what I want to hear. Or I will answer a question with a question so as to not really answer the question, a survival strategy that I learned but I'm not sure where. Most people don't pick up on it, but this man did. It was kind of funny to me, so every time we had a conversation after that startling revelation, he'd make me clarify what I was asking him. And then he'd be quick to justify his answers, as well.

So, what does this have to do with peace? Well, if I have had the peace of shalom, then I wouldn't have done these things. And now that I'm conscious of them, I have to ask God to give me His peace.

I often tell people I take them literally, at exactly what they say. I take them at their word. I don't care what you mean, because all I have is what you say. So, when talking with me, you must choose your words carefully. For example, if you ask me, "What's wrong with your head?" but you actually meant my hairstyle, I take it that there's something wrong with my head and not my hair. I don't understand or get jokes, and I often remind my friends not to bother telling them to me. The reason I usually don't get them is because jokes are not logical; they don't make sense to me. I will spend a lot of time analyzing the joke and miss the punch line totally. And on the rare occasion when someone tells me a joke, I find that sometimes it is so stupid that even I have to laugh. But for the most part, I find jokes to be cruel and berating. Think about the "joke" that you think is soooo funny—who is it hurting or berating? Women, blondes, people you know, people you don't know, short people, religious people? Who is that joke putting down?

I listen to the things people say to me. Oftentimes this disrupts my peace. So, I've learned to limit those whom I allow to pour into me and into my spirit. I limit people, the television, the radio, and most forms of media. I don't have a problem with turning it all off, putting it down, or walking away. The devil wants to invade and corrupt our communications and our privacy. Have you noticed when you're trying to study the Word of God, that suddenly out of nowhere you'll start thinking of something someone said or something else you could be doing? Or you find that you are so distracted that you can't study or pray at all. The devil's entire purpose is to steal your joy; he knows that faith comes by hearing, and hearing the Word of God (see Romans 10:17). Satan will try to infiltrate our subconscious mind in hopes of sabotaging our conscious mind. This is his attempt to sidetrack us from what God has ordained us to do. Those three monkeys we see—one with his eyes covered, one with his ears covered, and the last with his mouth covered—had a lot to say. Are you listening? Are you listening to what the Spirit has to say? Are you hearing what God has to say? Jesus has said that His sheep know His voice (see John 10:27). Do you know God's voice? Are you able to hear Him when He speaks to you? Have you studied enough? Have you meditated enough? Have you fasted enough? Are you willing to be broken? These things come by prayer and supplication. One without the other just won't do.

We often hear people say, "Don't let anyone steal your joy!" When our peace is disrupted, it takes away our joy. We are anxious, and the Bible warns us in Philippians 4:6 to *be anxious for nothing, but in everything, by prayer and supplication, with thanksgiving, let your re-*

quests be made known to God" (NKJV). So that tells me to seek peace from God, through prayer, while I am being grateful. It seems easy enough and simple, too; just go to God and ask.

God has promised us that He'll never leave us nor forsake us. He's promised that if we will just ask in His name, He will do it (see John14:13). And He says that He will supply all our needs according to His riches in glory (see Philippians 4:19). He's just waiting for us to ask. He says, *"Behold, I stand at the door and knock"* (see Revelation 3:20). Are we willing to open the door and let Him come in? He doesn't force Himself on us. He waits patiently for us to invite Him in.

Why not open your heart and let Him come in? He'll give you perfect peace. He'll give you the peace that surpasses all understanding, the peace of *shalom.* Jesus is that peace.

CPSIA information can be obtained
at www.ICGtesting.com
Printed in the USA
LVHW020605230920
666822LV00004B/399